When Journey
Becomes the Goal

When Journey Becomes the Goal

Success Through Personal Leadership

Mohit Tomar

PARTRIDGE
A Penguin Random House Company

Because of the dynamic nature of the Internet, any web addresses or links contained in this book may have changed since publication and may no longer be valid. The views expressed in this work are solely those of the author and do not necessarily reflect the views of the publisher, and the publisher hereby disclaims any responsibility for them.

Print information available on the last page.

To order additional copies of this book, contact
Partridge India
000 800 10062 62
orders.india@partridgepublishing.com

www.partridgepublishing.com/india

Contents

Contents

Dedicated to my grandmother, Mrs. Bohti Singh,
whose life has always been a source of inspiration to me.

Preface

Human life has a mazed layout, full of ambiguity and uncertainty, often leading us to perplexity and bewilderment. The directions to move on and decisions to take, are difficult and demanding. It needs some intuition and daring in this unique adventure. Management theories and tools snap while helping us to manage our life. Since we have not created life, we cannot form studies and strategies to deal with life.

The laboratory of life is unique for each of us and we have to go through our own individual crucible and non-crucible experiences. As such, we need personal leadership and learning to move on the journey of life. Life is essentially a leadership endeavor. It does not need a position or a protocol, but a purpose. A divine purpose.

This struggle and search for a purpose in life forms the very basis of human existence. Why are human beings' lives full of problems and difficulties? Why do we invite challenges? Such questions inspired me to write this book. I am not an author by profession and have just made a humble attempt to compile my reflections and contemplations on issues of life and how personal leadership can help us to deal with them.

In this book I have touched upon certain philosophical and practical approaches towards the journey of life. Although this book is for people of all ages, I hope that students and youth will gain some advantage from it, in finding a direction for their lives, and treat life as a platform for learning and leadership.

Foreword

I first met Capt. Mohit Tomar on a technical mountaineering course cum expedition organized by the Indian Ministry of Defence in 2014 in Uttarkashi, Uttarakhand. Given my business and technical background, such physically demanding activities have always been beyond my area of expertise. So I was quite excited and more than a little nervous. But there was nothing really to worry about. Capt. Mohit was such a calm, fine and a true teacher that he instantly put me at ease with his wit, humour and clarity of mind.

Because of his Army background and his disciplined lifestyle, he was not only physically far better conditioned than most trainees but also demonstrated exceptional leadership skills that instantly led him to being chosen as the Course Senior. Soon enough everyone could see how composed he remained and how completely comfortable he was in his shoes. He's just one of those persons you look forward to being with, whom you think about with a smile and a sense of admiration.

During that one month of complete isolation from rest of the world and ever since then, I have come to a realization that over a period of time and through his life altering experiences, Capt. Mohit has acquired a clear understanding about the peculiarities of human mind. He works very hard to use his understanding in helping his friends, students at ISL (Bangalore) and in general everyone around him to break the self-imposed boundaries established by them. These boundaries could pertain to anything ranging from love to career. It is because of these boundaries that we tend to get stuck in ourselves.

We spend our whole lives chasing love, money, success, power, groundbreaking business ideas, fame, and appreciation but little do we know whether this is something that we really want or is this something planted by our society on our minds. One may think that only these parameters alone can truly define an individual's happiness. Maybe they do temporarily. But eventually we just become scared, disappointed and frustrated. Deep in our minds we do recognize this but refrain from challenging what has already been established in textbooks. Even the autobiographies of the greatest people are a testimony to the fact that tales of those people who have lived a superficial life and with an unclear frame of mind have not made it to those coveted book shelves. The ones who did are the ones who dug deep and found what resonated with their soul. They accepted their weaknesses and built on their strengths.

With the help of this book, Capt. Mohit has attempted to encourage readers to examine their lives in connection with their society, life's problems, and their own ambitions.

Answers to questions such as – 'who we currently are?', 'how can we be what we originally wanted to be?' - can only be found in ourselves. This book does not claim to teach you a shortcut to success or preaches for you to be a 'super-human' but rather inspires you to see the bigger picture, accept that life is random and yet find that exact thing that resonates with your soul.

This path is not esoteric or requires some special ability. In fact it is easy. With this book the author hopes to ignite a spark in you that may eventually progress into a roaring flame. The power lies within you!

---- APAAR MAHAJAN
Mech. Engineer, MBA and Entrepreneur
University of Oxford, UK

1

Resonate with your 'Self'

"The unexamined life is not worth living."

— Socrates

The concept of life has been dealt with and delved in many ways and generated a plethora of fields of study. Still, it is the most intriguing and intricate concept to be understood by mankind.

Recently, I was in a school for a talk, and I overheard a teacher telling a student, 'If you can write it hundred times it does not mean that you understand it'. How true. Such is life, if we have lived through years, then it does not necessarily mean that we have understood the meaning and purpose behind life or to be more accurate, our lives. Why do we take birth? What are we here for? How do our lives matter? Where do we fit, in the big picture of the universe? Many such questions have inspired and instigated the mankind to reach higher and go farther. It is difficult to answer conclusively such questions, and the more we contemplate on these, the more confusing the situation becomes. But the human race is identified by a deep desire to understand the reason behind its existence. No other living entity has exhibited this innate quest.

"When I discover who I am, I'll be free."
— Ralph Ellison, Invisible Man

Essentially, all forms of life are about self-expression. We think, speak, and act, to express ourselves. In fact the entire human race, have been attempting to express itself over the centuries. We are intelligent enough to understand that death is our ultimate reality, but this does not deter us from dreaming and daring. We know that we have to leave everything behind, but still we build and re-build.

As a trainer, often I have often been asked to guide the younger generation to enable them to choose the right career, do well in their profession and to live an effective and successful life. I wonder how easy life could have been if there had been a check-list of things to do and criteria for success. If there had been a system, strategy or a structure for a successful living. But every life is unique and rolls out a unique path to follow. Each life has its own meaning and purpose and the essence of all our endeavor should be to find it. Life cannot have a universal template. We all are unique and have to live unique lives. Lives cannot be photocopies.

The essence of all training and teachings lies in asking the right questions. Initially it may lead to dissonance but this is essential for our long term resonance within and with-out. Actually we do not need answers. Answers will pop up on their own once we ask the right questions of ourselves. It is the right questions which give us right direction on the journey of our life.

What is right direction?

The right direction is essentially the one which brings peace, prosperity and permanence; not only for us but for all. It is what makes us happy and that which we would love to not only live for but die for. It is the idea, concept or reason to live, in which we find the purpose of our existence. It gives us resonance inside and outside. We just feel happy doing it. Our involvement or engagement in it, is itself a reward for us.

We all must have read a book, met a person, watched a movie, attended a lecture, worked on an idea and so on, which just makes us feel good and we feel a burst of energy and emotions from it. We feel some inner voice and thinks 'this is what I think' or 'this is what I should do'. It is our 'aha' moment. We feel a sense of self-expression. This is the time to stop and think, and to decide the direction of our life or at least the directives of our unique lives.

The outside world can give us methods and measures to deal with our journey but it is our inside world which provides the purpose and meaning of our journey, As such, outside guidance and suggestions hold little value when they do not fit with one's inner world. It is imperative that we delve deep into ourselves through right questions and listen to our inner voice.

The inner voice is subtle and feeble and can only be heard through deep self-awareness. All outside noise has to be curtailed to listen to the inner voice. We are blessed to be born in the present Information age when every piece of information, instruction, and insight is available only a few simple clicks away on the internet. Our life is easy to an extent but at the same time complicated and confused in a big way. In today's busy and bizarre world, often, we often have too much knowledge but too little understanding. All around us, we find people engrossed and 'entangled' with their cellphones, tablets, laptops, and other communication devices, which leaves them little time to think, reflect and contemplate. Too much dependency on external aids has not only obstructed our mind but also retarded our social skills, where we do not make friends' but add friends' to our friends' lists. Sadly, we do not have any 'software application' which can help us to connect with ourselves.

> "Your visions will become clear only when you can look into your own heart. Who looks outside, dreams; who looks inside, awakes."
> — C.G. Jung

The inner voice is the compass for our journey of life. We need to know ourselves through a series of outside experiences and inner conversations, to know ourselves and find our right direction.

So what should we do?

Know yourself. Know the world around you. Find the interconnectedness in the world. Do not make an effort to know yourself. Knowing oneself is a subtle journey and cannot have a prescribed path. Do not react or respond, just feel and listen. Do not try to justify or put things in the grid of right and wrong. (Of course, as long as it is not unethical and illegal). Putting effort here is like struggling in the quicksand. The harder we work the quicker we drown. Do not apply logic and reasoning, since it is relative and there is no universal logic or reasoning. Age old wisdom of mankind has been defied and upgraded through the evolution of mankind, in its own unique and natural way.

In my life, when I got ideas, like climbing Mount Everest, joining Army or changing my profession, I never questioned them and just gave in. Most people, especially those who cared for me, tried to stop me from doing it. But I am happy that I listened to my inner voice and moved on my unique journey. Since we all are unique individuals with unique souls, then it is unjust to consult others as to what to do and why a person should choose a particular endeavor or enterprise for his life. Guidance and suggestions regarding 'how' may be taken from experts or others who have proved their excellence in a field. But what journey to take is a not even a personal but spiritual decision and has to be taken through self-awareness and self- responsibility.

> "I think....you still have no idea. The effect you can have."
> — Suzanne Collins, Mockingjay

Life is difficult because we can think. It is important to follow a path of endeavors as per the grain of our soul. It is crucial to recognize our 'unique' disposition which can be achieved through a state of mindlessness where all thinking ceases and our inner voice is heard. Deep introspection, and interaction with self is crucial to find our true selves. Gaining outside knowledge helps us to deal with outside world, but to live in peace with self, we need a deep self-knowledge or self-awareness.

What is life's journey?

Life is essentially an interaction between the man's inner and outer world. We all live on this interface between our inside and outside world. This interaction and interface between us and our environment defines us. We are essentially an extension of our inner self, our true self. But at the present time, we are so busy in the outer world that we are not left with enough time and resources to look within us. In digging up millions of websites, we find little time to dig deep within ourselves.

Life's journey is about matching our inner and outer world. Whatever we feel within us, we search for it or act to create it in the outside world. We search for friends, books, movies, professions, hobbies and so on, which resonates with our inner environment. We act relentlessly on ideas and dreams that emanate from deep within.

What gives us self-awareness?

Firstly, a life is a dynamic entity and keeps changing, growing, developing and evolving every moment, as such, it is not a one-time affair. We need to interact with and interrogate ourselves on a regular basis, to be updated about the latest developments within. Secondly, life is messy and nonsensical, and difficult to understand. It has always been a human struggle to find sense in this nonsense. Thirdly, we cannot gain self-awareness in isolation, we need to study ourselves in relation to our surroundings.

Whether life is an accident or a purposeful event, the thought has always intrigued me and I have never achieved any progress in this quest. But I realized that it is both. It depends on us, what we want to make out of it. Life, per se has no meaning, till such time as we give a meaning to it.

Just as we conduct so many experiments with different chemicals, to know their properties and prospective uses, we need to expose ourselves to a variety and vast range of experiences and events to know our true selves. We need to experiment with selves to know our true natures, to nurture ourselves for any prospective use of our qualities. Self-awareness is not gained through routine but through risk-taking. Tests and trials of life are like mirror to reflect our true images to us. We need

> "We must do that which we think we cannot."
> -- Eleanor Roosevelt, first lady

to find patterns and trends to our liking and longing to know our true selves, only then we can move further on the journey of life.

Why to gain self-awareness?

To resonate with self. To live at peace and live one's passion. Knowledge about self provides us our purpose.

One can drive a car if one knows the basic functions of driving but if we have knowledge about its mechanism, we can surely drive well and avoid problems regarding breakdowns and malfunctioning. For the same reason, in aviation, where the stakes are higher, pilots have a detailed knowledge about the aircraft and aerodynamics along with their flying skills. Similarly, for a human being, a deep knowledge about self will make living a passion filled and purposeful experience and will make him transcend from mere existence to evolution.

One's 'self' is the basic instrument or tool with which we live, work or play. Then how can we imagine to living a worthy life without knowing ourselves? We are not born to live but to flourish, flower and bear fruit. If a person knows his self, he can move ahead in harmony with himself. Tuning in with oneself is possible, when we know our frequency.

> "To say "I love you" one must know first how to say the "I"."
> — Ayn Rand, The Fountainhead

We can tune in and listen to pleasant music, only when we know what is being broadcast and what we like. Outside knowledge becomes powerful and productive when it is resonates with self-knowledge.

The journey of gaining knowledge should be two directional 'with-out' and from 'with-in'. If we keep gaining outside knowledge with little heed to our true selves, our souls, then we are bound to go into imbalance. Alignment with self can only lead us to our purpose. Today, we find people who, after being successful in their profession, discover themselves to be failures and frustrated. Success is truly our alignment with our divine purpose. As such, if we are growing and gaining knowledge outside, we need to do the same 'with-in' too. If our actions do not fit into the journey of life or the 'big picture' we have decided for ourselves, then we are surely going to feel discouraged and dejected in the near future.

Due to easy access to information, today we know about every nook and corner of the world, but have little understanding of ourselves and also of our immediate environment, culture, customs and traditions. This really is a big problem of the day where people are facing severe identity crises, and the chaotic environment. Problems such as job dissatisfaction and marriage breakdowns are gifts of this new order (or disorder) of the day. A reference point is required by everyone, to fall back on and to launch from, in terms of our thoughts, decisions and actions. Without this, we lose our sense of security and stability. Even countries and institutions, have constitutions which guide us in difficult and different times, then where is our personal constitution for references and recommendations. The power of purpose is immense and gives us our direction and destination.

Thinking global and acting local, is a key to live in the present era where geographical and cultural boundaries have diffused. Even if one wants to bring changes in society, it is not from out to in but vice versa. A deep respect and recognition of self and our immediate culture and customs is crucial to live a happy and fruitful life. Self-awareness and awareness about our world can only help us to achieve it.

How does self-awareness help?

Self-awareness is a divine gift, but sadly, majority of the people never achieve it. Divine intervention is important in this process. It transcends out present life and helps us to discover our purpose or more rightly, help us to create our purpose.

Happiness or 'Anandam' is not about any material gain, it surpasses all tangibles and enlightens us about those intangibles which cannot be destroyed but are permanent, profound and pervasive. This is the only true form of happiness, when we are beyond pain and pleasure, when we are in love with self and the universe. It takes us into a 'trance' where nothing else matters. People may call such a person 'crazy' and we all know that a little 'craziness' was behind all the greatest works of art, literature, science, social reforms, or any other kind of development.

However, the journey to self-awareness is not easy, and we cannot just sit and gain it. It happens through the tiring and tortuous route of experiences, reflections and contemplation. Let us examine this process in detail.

Firstly, we misunderstand events as experiences. We all go through events every day and every time but they become experiences only when we think about them. Secondly, experiences need to be severe and shocking to really shake us. Not only does 'pain purify the soul' but also aesthetics, in any form, comes through pain. A caterpillar turns into a butterfly through a painful metamorphosis. A beautiful body is also a result of long and strenuous hours spent in a gymnasium. Similarly, to own an evolved and enlightened soul, we need to go through crisis and chaos. A sense of aesthetics develops from messiness and vagueness. Even the scientific research papers which look so crisp and concise, are produced through a long series of experiments and re-experimentation and a messy journey of trial and errors. To evolve, we need to go through a journey of experiences and finding our right frequency. Only then we can calibrate ourselves with outside world and live in resonance with self. Resonance not only multiplies our energy to the maximum level and sets us in a 'flow', but it also provides us a deep sense of satisfaction and pleasure. Flow is the ultimate communion with in ourselves and with our environment when we feel a great burst of energy and we get enough power to achieve the unimaginable. In scientific terms, we like music with a certain frequency which matches with our own biological clock, as it leads to resonance and gives a pleasant feeling.

> "Experience is valuable only if it's imbued with meaning from which one can draw salient conclusions. Otherwise, experience becomes imprisoning."
> -- Barry McCaffrey, general

Once we know our 'frequency' we can know our true 'calling'. Only then can we realize which problems we are here to solve and what use we can be to the humanity and most importantly ourselves. Our experiences do change us, but through self-awareness we can have control of our lives, and master the ability to respond to and retain the insights gained from our experiences.

All the ancient scriptures, focus a great deal on the journey with-in and 'meeting with self'. Even Aristotle, mentor to world's most famous conqueror, Alexander, truly conveyed the bottom line of a purposeful living, when he said, 'Know thyself, Control thyself, and Give thyself'. In others words, first travel within, know who you are and what you are here for, then discipline yourself to convert your latent self into a skill and finally liberate it, to add value to this world.

A human being, or even a culture or country reaches its zenith when it starts living a way of life, which liberates, which enables exploration within, experiment with self, and matures one to the fullest potential. When we start doing things which appeal to us and our environment, then the journey overrides the quest for any specific and measurable goal. Every moment becomes pleasant and purposeful. At that stage, goal achievement is no more a criterion for success. For instance, living a life of integrity is a journey, a way of life and is not attained through a particular goal.

If someone loves music, it hardly matters how many famous tunes one has played, if through playing music one can find solace and peace. If one likes to run and his soul gets pleasure in it, then timing does not matter. When a person has something to share from the heart, he is by default, a writer or a speaker. If one loves a person, then the feeling cannot be proved through any goal. If one believes in and lives for a cause or a belief, then we do not need to bother about a goal, our sheer love and living for it will improve us and give peace to our soul.

Life is a journey...

To find true success in life, first we need to define life. Life is essentially a confusing concept and we need to delve further into its meaning. It is a phase of time that we are here to spend, as physical entities. As such, it's a journey. We live and last when we live as 'travelers'. Whoever completes this journey has solved the purpose of his existence. We need to experience all the flavors of living to live a wholesome and worthwhile life. If pleasure is important, pain also has meaning, we need to be confused to get clarity, no one has succeeded if he has not failed enough. We cannot choose the outcome of our decisions, but only the decisions. Indifferent to results, we can decide how we want to live our lives.

One name which always manifests as the true example of a journey well completed, is that of King Asoka the Great, who qualifies to be the greatest king in India history. Under his rule in the third century BC, the Mauryan kingdom reached its maximum heights of sovereignty and prosperity. Asoka's last battle was the battle of Kalinga, in which

> "Winning is important to me, but what brings me real joy is the experience of being fully engaged in whatever I'm doing."
> -- Phil Jackson, basketball coach

lakhs of people were killed. However, after winning everything, he experienced a sense of loss and grief within. The loss of life on such a large scale shocked him to the core and he realized the futility in his victory. He underwent a transition, which changed the course of his journey and set a new order in history.

He found the futility in abundance, a sense of loss after winning, who discovered himself after losing himself. When his journey was completed, the distinction and difference was lost between winning and losing, pain and pleasure, pride and repentance, big and small, and at last he won himself by surrendering. He became powerful by being powerless. Thereafter he worked towards the highest goal of life….moving on a path of purpose…to bestow this world with peace and prosperity, compassion and care….and he left a legacy of long-lasting love. He truly lived a life where his journey became the goal.

The pursuit of Happiness

Happiness is definitely not a state of mind. Happiness without a reason is a symptom of insanity. As humans, we need some specific reasons to be happy. Happiness cannot be pursued as a goal, only the reasons which makes us happy can be sought. Living our life from 'true self,' in alignment with our reasons and beliefs, is a journey of happiness. When we do something in which we find a meaning or a purpose, it makes us happy, no matter how much trouble and tribulations we have to go through.

The moment we discover an endeavor in which we find a purpose, the reason behind our unique existence, we rise above all problems and predicaments, and start enjoying our lives. We achieve an eternal bliss. It is like a meditation and people may call us 'crazy' but we feel content and gratified. But to know our purpose, we need to know 'self'.

Happiness is not the absence of difficulties, as even the sense of accomplishment by overcoming difficulties gives us happiness. Challenges are essential to our existence, they gives us self-awareness and self-mastery. In fact we take on challenges to achieve happiness happy. Ability to accept and overcome challenges denotes the health of a human being.

> "The greatest thing in the world is to know how to belong to oneself."
> — Michel de Montaigne, The Complete Essays

A happy person is full of clarity. His mind is devoid of any contradictions and confusions. A happy person knows what he is doing and why he is doing it. He has very clear reasoning and philosophy behind his life and living. He is living his life from within, his natural being. He does not do anything today, which he does not want to do tomorrow. It is very common to hear people saying, 'I do not want to be in this job' (but still they struggle in the same job), 'I wish I could have pursued my hobby' (but still they never make an efforts towards it), 'I do not want much money' (but still they toil every day to earn) and so on. It is quintessential to first clarify to ourselves what we really want. Otherwise we feel revolt within us, as our soul is not heard. We crumble from inside and go into depression and dejection. Great empires have not fallen due to some major attacks from without, but mostly due to imbalance and implosion within. In words of one of our nation's idols, Ratan Tata, 'Iron destroys on its own through the process of rusting'.

When we love doing what we do or we do what we love, the journey itself becomes worth it. Every step on it provides value, and we do not need assessment of failure and success.

Every life born on this earth is itself a success and as such, all its unique qualities and endeavors are in themselves a success.

If we look at all great personalities, they found and fulfilled a particular purpose in their lives. They discovered and developed on their passion. Their lives were not a routine of existence but a service to their own purpose. Life is not about reaching any particular destination. It is about direction, where every moment and movement is a destination.

"To be what we are, and to become what we are capable of becoming, is the only end in life."

Robert Louis Stevenson

2

Fail Often

Far better is it to dare mighty things, to win glorious triumphs, even though checkered by failure... than to rank with those poor spirits who neither enjoy nor suffer much, because they live in a gray twilight that knows not victory nor defeat.

Theodore Roosevelt

Failure has always been a taboo in our society, we do not want to fail. As we grow, a false sense of pride and perfection sets in, and we resist failing. We always want to be right. In fact, at times we stop deciding and acting, so as not be wrong. Any failure hurts our ego and humiliates us. We do not want to fail, and want to be perfect every time. However, history is privy to the fact that whenever mankind has made a mistake or failed, it ushered itself into new unexplored territories of geography, science, art, philosophy and literature.

Since life is a journey, a single or end event of producing results is not the true criteria of success. The experience of charm, creativity, chaos and character invested in the process to achieve the end result is the real reward. As someone has said, it is not what you get out of it but what you become in the process. Since the end goal of all human endeavor is to evolve and set new standards, then why worry about results, as long as it brings growth to ourselves and our society. As long as it is bringing us a new order of thinking and acting, it is worth it. As humans we never fail, we always grow and gain from our attempts, we always evolve through our mistakes and failures. Failures are only failures in the outside world when our performance is short of an expectation or expected result. However, inside us, every failure brings in a new order through new questions and queries.

It is the messy process of trials and errors, failures and successes, hope and despair, pain and pleasure, which develops us. If we love what we do and find a sense of purpose in what we do, then every moment is worth relishing. What better life, can a man live, than one in which he does what he loves doing and loves what he does. When a person does not mind failing or succeeding in doing something that is his true calling.

Today, our society, workplace, and family, determines our success by goal-sheets which greatly underestimates and undermines true human potential, which gets discovered and developed only through failures. Greatest discoveries and inventions are results of wild imaginations, strong-headed initiatives and pure intentions. But where is the criteria to measure these.

Trial and error is a natural way to grow and flourish. A child cannot learn to walk without falling, a shooter cannot become a marksman without missing targets, and scientific inventions cannot be evolved without tests and trials. History is full of instances of repeated failures as a prelude to excellence. Even great personalities have been born out of failures. The early failures of their lives gave them a balanced and better perspective of life.

> "It's failure that gives you the proper perspective on success." - Ellen DeGeneres

What happens when we fail?

We ask questions, we think, when we fail. Failure agitates us, hurts us and stimulates us. We get into confusion and chaos, things become foggy with no clear path, our notions and skills do not help us and we start questioning and re-thinking. Revolution starts, of course first within us and then outside us. The more we question, the more clarity we get.

Life is not about answering right but questioning right. Asking the right questions happens when things go wrong and existing methods do not work. Questioning sets on a journey. Every time we fail, we get frustrated but it takes us to a new level of living. Life is essentially a process of discovering, what works and what does not, this happens through failing.

Every time I failed badly, I got renewed and reformed, as it led me to know the limitations of my beliefs, knowledge and skills, and guided me to review my action. It confused me through a series of questions. For instance, what was my fault?, why did it happen to me?, what could I have done?, how could I have handled it better?, how would I respond, if similar things happen again?.

> "If you're not prepared to be wrong, you'll never come up with anything original." - Ken Robinson

The more severe and stark the experience, the more simple and strict the questions we start to ask. Why do I even exist on this earth? Is everything predefined and pre-decided or is it a consequence of our actions? Do we have control of our lives?

How to fail?

Fail with grace and élan. See the big picture and how the event fits into it. Go with the flow. It is time to reflect and contemplate and make conclusions. Every bitter experience should bring out the best in us. Success is not the opposite of failure but the end of journey of failures, or more rightly, the journey through failures.

To grow and evolve, we need to fail in an organized and ordained manner. Failures without reflection, records and revisions does not take us anywhere. They provide us learning only when we think and deliberate on them.

Inculcating the attitude and ability to deal with failures should be an essential part of our school and college education curriculum. Children should be taught to experiment with different ideas and concepts even in face of failure. Generally, the stalwarts of entrepreneurship had not performed well through school and college. They possess a very different kind of mental toughness and creative instinct to deal with failures. Failures do not lead them to suicide or depression. They are used to failing and do not need to safeguard any record of achievements. They have nothing to lose and this nothingness gives them the courage to take new risks and experiment with new ideas. They truly make life an adventure.

I personally suggest that every day we must do something where we may fail, if we intend to grow. But it is essential that we fail responsibly. We should

> "Let me be wrong for some time and let us see where it takes me."
> -- Mohit Tomar

have the intention and initiative to respond as we wish, in times of failure. We must take failures as a way of life. I always wonder, what is wrong in failing, as long as it is providing us its benefits? No wisdom requires that we should always be right.

How does failing helps us?

Failures purifies us and builds our character. Pain purifies the soul. Difficult times develops our character. Just like a footballer gets trained on a football field, an actor hones his skills on stage, the character is built through crucible experiences. The times of failure are difficult times, which give a better and bigger picture of self, and adds brilliance to our schema and spectra. It enriches our inner programming and outward behavior.

Every failure poses a different level of frustration and fatigue. Failures generally result in some kind of loss either financial, time, peace of mind, respect and effort, to name a few. It really needs courage and consistent efforts to turn around. In the process, we find a new order within us. We evolve or metamorphose in to a new being, much more peaceful, productive and pleasant.

Being from a sales background, I fully understand the value of rejections in the process of reaching the right clients. The rejections are never pleasant but that is the principle of selling and we need to abide by it. What keeps one moving ahead is one's belief in the product or service and one's intention to help people through it.

> "Character consists of what you do on the third and fourth tries."
> -- James Michener, Author

When to fail?

Failure is necessary and we cannot avoid it but we can decide the timing and intensity in order to avoid high stakes. It is appropriate for a cyclist to try cycling on a cycle and fall before balance. On the other hand, a pilot needs to fail many times in the simulator before getting on to a real flight. Tolerance for failing in training needs can be high, to avoid losses in the real scenario.

The goal of all education should be to develop humans to their fullest potential. As such, it is imperative to create a culture of making more mistakes and errors in order to find the right answer. The perception of always giving right answers and getting good marks, may hinder a child from doing anything new, to avoid failure. Just to be right every time, such a student produces the previously recorded information without bringing one's unique understanding and approach to a problem. In the end, such students, stop taking risks and trying new things, so as not to fail. They remain an asset to their organization no longer, as they cannot bring anything new to the table. Their experience and credentials become their liabilities.

Our greatness lies in being born as a humans, in the first place. As humans we are endowed with the ability to think and also to think about our thinking. We have full capability to respond and react to any situation in the way we want. Failures, big or small, strengthen our human nature every time and helps us to develop to our full maturity.

> "Only those who dare to fail greatly can ever achieve greatly." - Robert F. Kennedy

The only way to avoid failures and frustrations is to do nothing and be nothing. Only one man has no problems in life, the one who is in the grave. Life is a package of successes and failures.

Life is hope. Recently, at Everest Base Camp, while attempting the summit of Mt. Everest, I witnessed one of the worst earthquakes Nepal has had. The base camp was beautiful site, where at a height of 18,000 feet, men have stocked a cache of human tools and toys. The place was vibrant and vigorous with dreams and daring of a large number of climbers. I had been preparing for this expedition for a year, through a strenuous and strict regime. But it took less than a minute, by God to destroy all. All efforts by the man, were ripped apart. Men, dead and injured, and other material were all spread over the glacier. A human being is wired in a crazy way. Nothing can diminish and destroy the human spirit. Every time a human endeavor has failed, he has risen again, with more determination and grit. The instinct to re-build is deep routed and deep entrenched. This is the beauty of being human. At that time, I realized not only the limitations of human in front of the mighty nature but also the limitless daunting and daring within him.

Growth occurs when we move out of our comfort zone but it also poses unknown risks and requirements. When our present knowledge and skills does not equip us to deal with the situation, we are bound to fail, but it is the only way to grow. The failure leads us into a state of agitation and action to enrich and enlarge ourselves with updated knowledge and skills. We recalibrate and relaunch ourselves. Challenging oneself is the basic human nature and one seeks to challenge oneself with new tasks. In fact, it is not an exaggeration to say that lack of challenge itself is a form of torture to the human spirit, as we are naturally wired to flourish and bloom under challenges.

Even while recruiting an employee in a firm, selecting a student for admission, or finding a life partner, the important criterion to be considered is "How many times has the person failed?", "How has he handled his failures?", "How much has he evolved in the process?". In fact the extent of our journey on the path of trials and errors, is a direct indication of the level of our evolution.

All the current tools and equipment around us are in the present version after a long journey of improvements and innovation, which happened when they failed to meet the new needs of the user. Even knowledge and wisdom, which mankind possesses in the present age have gone through a tortuous path of tests, trials and tribulations in order to answer human questions.

Why we fear failure?

It is the feelings and perception associated with failure that bother us and we refrain from attempting new challenges. The adventurous spirit of entrepreneurship, exploring, experiment and endurance is largely a function of our cultural background. Most discoveries and inventions happened in some particular region of the world and in a particular era.

If we encourage our employees, students and children to fail and relieve them of all the stigma associated with failure, then the human race will evolve to a new level. Today, certain companies create a culture of attempts to ideate and invent, even in face of failures. Failures are rewarded and are recognized as a step towards success and standards of performance. No doubt, such companies survived the worst financial recessions. They are able to provide upgraded products and services, apply new methodologies and practices, and relate and respond to the new settings.

> "Maturity, one discovers, has everything to do with the acceptance of 'not knowing.'"
> — Mark Z. Danielewski, House of Leaves

Interestingly, by birth or basic nature, we are not afraid of failing. Children playing and engaging in different activities are a direct indication of this fact. They are not afraid of failing and love to try new things or new ways of doing things. That is why maximum learning happens in initial years of our lives and we learn how to live in the 'setting' of this world. We adapt, adjust and accommodate to the social, scientific and other survival norms of the world. However, as we grow and our ego takes shape, a false sense of vanity is established in us and we start resisting failure.

Mostly, in face of failures and setbacks, our credibility is doubted and we are inhibited in taking initiative. We also face self-doubt. As a result, we abhor the idea of failing. However, failures are necessary stepping stones towards success and this principle cannot be denied.

What helps us to deal with failures?

In times of failure, apart from culture, an individual's character plays a crucial role for him to re-collect himself, re-assess, re-organize and re-launch. Character itself is developed in the crucible of challenges. Character cannot be developed through books and lectures but by taking the difficult path of practicing natural principles of life. Above all, a love for life and its lessons, goes a long way to move steadily on the journey of life, even in face of failures. When the aim of all human endeavor is to improve and transform humanity, then there is no need to fear failure because the journey itself becomes the goal. When we love our journey and the purpose it is rooted in, we relish each phase, both failures and successes.

What doesn't kill you only makes you stronger. When we fail, we automatically raise the threshold level of our endurance for the rest of our lives. It may appear like the end of the world at the time, but next time a setback of an equal magnitude may seem nothing more than a mild hiccup.

Success is important to know what works, and equally, failure is important to know what does not work. To live a balanced life the criticality of each cannot be denied. A well-rounded and well-groomed personality is one who has a share of each. Ironically, we only see the success and positive credentials of a candidate in different spheres of life, but at none of the times do we inquire about how often he failed and the lessons he learnt. We never check his ability to deal with failures, his mental toughness and resilience. Generally the people with most successful journeys are the first ones to snap under the difficult times of failures, when everything is clouded and confusing. Only a person who can see the meaning in failures and possess 'failure credentials' can be an asset, in dealing with difficult situations.

Failures and bounce-backs provide us inspiration

Even our inspiration does not come from a journey of only successes, only but by the stories of ups and downs in a person's life and how he bounced back every time. The elasticity and endurance displayed in a character is the real source of inspiration. It proves that we are naturally wired to fail and bounce back.

Among so many such names, Abraham Lincoln, the sixteenth President of United States, is one which such figure

> Success is how high you bounce when you hit bottom.
> George S. Patton

who has inspired generation through his sheer grit and determination. His mettle of character was proved through a series of failures and his re-attempts every time. He proved the essential belief of human life….hope.

Born into abject poverty, Abraham Lincoln had to face difficulties and defeat throughout his life. He lost eight elections, failed in two businesses, and suffered a nervous breakdown, which left him bedridden for six months.

A list of Lincoln's failures:

- 1832 - Lost Job, defeated in elections to state legislature
- 1833 - Business he started fails
- 1835 - Personal love interest (Ann Rutledge) dies
- 1836 - Suffers from nervous breakdown
- 1838 - Defeated after running for Illinois House Speaker
- 1843 - Defeated in nomination to Congress
- 1848 - Lost re-nomination to Congress
- 1854 - Defeated in his run for Senate, 1854
- 1856 - Defeated in his nomination for Vice President
- 1858 - Defeated in run for Senate

Despite such a history of failures, in 1860 Lincoln was elected President and proved to be one of the greatest presidents in US history. His far-sightedness and forethought brought peace and prosperity for all. Through his faith in equality, and campaign for abolishing the malpractices such as slavery, he established one of the most stable and sustainable democracies of the world.

So, how can we say that failures are not good? All major re-evolutions are entrenched in failures.

"A man may fulfill the objective of his existence by asking a question he cannot answer and attempting a task he cannot achieve."

-- Oliver Wendell Holmes Sr., physician

3

Be Inspired

"It is a peculiarity of man that he can only live by looking to the future. And this is his salvation in the most difficult moments of his existence, although he sometimes has to force his mind to the task."

-- Viktor Frankl, Austrian Neurologist

Great works are not produced by diligence and discipline alone but through inspiration. The essence of human life is in its ability to get inspired and inspire others. No other animal on earth is endowed with this unique characteristic. Everyone works hard in today's competitive world but only a few people reach great heights. Why? Most of us do not have an inspiration. Only when our effort and endurance is motivated by inspiration, do we produce great work.

What is inspiration?

The term originates from the French word *Inspiracion* which means 'to breathe life into someone' and today it connotes the process of giving hope or igniting someone to action. It is anything which stimulates us to a higher level of energy and enthusiasm and primes us for action. It is a spiritual process, where something clicks and connects with us from deep within ourselves. We start living and operating at a higher level of existence.

We can be good under motivation, but great only under inspiration. Anything which gives us hope and happiness is a source of inspiration to us. It gives us a sense of purpose. Most people are dead at twenty five and buried at seventy five, due to a monotony forced upon them without the drive of inspiration. They live their lives routinely with all the excitement and exhilaration missing. However, the ideal way of living is an inspired life.

Even a dead man wakes up if he is inspired!

An inspired person is in a state of constant meditation. He feels he is in a trance and is one to one with himself and his work. Failing and passing a criterion does not matter to him, he transcends the present standards of excellence and is elevated to create or do something to express himself,

> A hero is someone who has given his or her life to something bigger than oneself.
> -Joseph Campbell

his unique talent. He himself become his critic and coach, and experiences a divine intervention. He sets new standards and straightens out new paths to follow for generations to come. He changes the order of the day.

How to get inspired?

Inspiration to human soul is as natural as eating, playing and working to our body and mind. We just need to live a natural way of life by finding the natural grain of our personality. Without judging or assessing, just listen to and live with the inner self. Do not use logic to listen to the heart. Logic has limitations and a shelf life. Hundred and fifty years back it was illogical to fly from Delhi to New

York but not today. What was logical yesterday is not logical today. So liberate yourself from the logics of the day, to listen to the divine voice within. Most of the times, we do not work upon our ideas or insights because they do not fit in the logics of the day. We think in terms of failure and success, or rejection and acceptance.

Find a pattern in your likes and dislikes, things doing which you lose track of time and you feel inner bliss, concepts and beliefs that you are comfortable with, people you like to spend time with, things you like to talk about at length with anyone, and so on. Be open-minded and liberate yourself without, harnessing your thoughts. Deep study of self, in terms of your thinking and actions, can give an insight into what inspires you.

Expose yourself to rich varieties of experiences. This enriches and enlarges your character and personality by giving you a better picture of self and naturally you tune into your inspiration. Traveling to different places, meeting new people, reading a variety of books, joining voluntary social work projects, playing different sports, learning new skills and above all, taking up new challenges in life are some of the ways to find your inspiration. You have to explore within and 'with-out'.

Inspiration cannot be borrowed or bought, it has to be discovered. It is a personal signature and defines our very

> We become what we think about.
> –Earl Nightingale

being. It gives insight about our uniqueness and universality.

It is our true identity and defines our relationship to the universe. It is a form of self-expression.

Being from a military background I enjoy watching military movies as they stimulate me to the core. Special missions and their demand for ultimate courage, camaraderie and cost makes me cry and contemplate for days. They cause me to see human life in a different light and provides an insight into human life's basic architecture.....why we just do not live like other animals who only seek survival and safety. Surely humans must live beyond this.

What inspiration gives us?

Today's management thinking has dealt with 'head' and 'hands' of human beings. The human resource is assessed in terms of its cognitive capabilities and physical fitness, or broadly its ability to perform and produce. But what about the 'heart'? Great pieces of art, scientific breakthroughs, social reforms, and sports records are achieved when one puts his or her heart into it. 'Why' and 'what' comes from 'heart', only the 'how' part is catered to by the 'head' and 'hand'. As such, it is imperative to harness the immense latent power of heart, where our inspiration and passion lies.

One can buy or force the hand and head but not the heart of people. To employ or associate ignited and inspired individuals we need to tap into the feelings of people. The real

> "To succeed, you need to find something to hold on to, something to motivate you, something to inspire you."
> -- Tony Dorsett, American Football Player

power lies in the emotion and feelings, which is the seat of our inspiration. Logic and reason do not inspire us, it is the stimulation of emotions which happens when something inside us resonates with something outside.

Whenever the boundary of human evolution or endeavor has been extended to new limits, an inspired being has been the root cause. Any institution or organization should create a culture around inspired people. These self-driven and self-critical people are the agents of change and apply standards of excellence. They can work consistently and courageously towards 'impossible' goals. They are never demotivated and dejected, even in face of failure.

Recently, I visited an engineering college where I was 'hooked' on the gallery of the Mechanical Department, where pictures, descriptions and works of stalwarts of mechanical engineering were displayed. I spent major time in reading and understanding their journey, with regard to their ingenuity, inventiveness and insights. Their passion, sacrifices and beliefs really inspired me. I realized that the subject itself has no meaning, but its association with human life and its emotions, is the critical source of our interest and inspiration.

Lee Kuan Yew, the architect and leader of Singapore is a great inspirational figure, who transformed Singapore from the verge of extinction to one

> Life is about making an impact, not making an income.
> –Kevin Kruse

of the most prosperous countries in the world. Today, this small island country stands out on the global map in terms of economy, culture and education. It is not Singapore's prosperity and peace which inspires but the imagination, vision, sacrifice and toil of the great leader which stimulates our emotions, to get us inspired. Through his leadership, Lee Kuan Yew gave a dream to every human in Singapore, an emotional dream, which made everyone work with high moral standards and ethics. Inspiration lets us break the barriers of our present existence and tests our limits. An inspired person inspires others and revolutionizes the ways of living and longing.

What inspires us?

A cause, an idea, personality, book, movie and quotes, among others could be the tools of inspiration. No logic works in it, as it just resonates with our souls. It goes beyond being apt or abrupt. It is not the cold concept which inspires us but its ability to stir our emotions to dream and dare.

Alexander the Great was inspired at an early age by his mentor, Aristotle with the idea of integrating the world. The idea of creating amusement parks for families and friends where they can spend quality time, was materialized by Walt Disney. The idea of freedom, where a person can live a life of dignity, led the legendary, Bhagat Singh to choose to die as a free man rather than live in captivity of the Birtish.

Anything to which we relate in a positive and productive manner can be a source of inspiration to us. It gives us a sense of an ideal state and the thing to strive for. It leads us to massive action.

Personally, I am inspired by movies, on great lives, ventures and missions where people opt to make their supreme sacrifices, and have changed the way we think forever. Being an avid reader, books have always been my true companion, and the stories, anecdotes, analogies and metaphors has always inspired me.

'Bravo Two Zero' is a book that stands out on this front because I can relate to the resilience of the human spirit as described in the narrative. In this book, the author Andy McNab, an ex-sergeant of the British SAS, recounts his mission in the Gulf War, when he with his team was dropped deep behind the enemy lines and were compromised. His struggle through escape and evasion, and torture as POW, displays the power of human determination and grit. It gave me the learning that 'people may break you physically but when you break mentally is totally your choice' and this message has helped me to sail through dark times in my own life.

How to inspire others?

During my tenure in army, one of my key result areas was to inspire my troops so that they could operate professionally and be constantly motivated. Only inspiration can help one to be happy in those high stress terrains and tasks. I had to lead

> "Keep your fears to yourself, but share your inspiration with others."
> -- Robert Louis Stevenson, writer

and set a personal example to them in order to help them survive and sustain the severity of military service. Above all, only an inspired person can inspire others. So before I could inspire others, I had to be an inspired person myself. It is not to be conveyed or communicated, but felt by people.

A single source of inspiration can activate a common man to achieve anything...literally anything.

When I heard General Arjun Ray, a veteran solder cum scholar and an educational reformist, saying, 'We do not conquer mountains, but climb to conquer ourselves, to purify ourselves", it just registered with me. I just felt something, a sense of calling. The emotions generated are difficult to put into words. I realized there is nothing to understand or scrutinize about it through my limited logic. I submitted to the inner calling and decided to attempt the summit of Mt. Everest. I had no idea of the planning and preparation that was ahead of me. But due to my strong belief and confidence, everything conspired to support me. Since the inspiration was not a planned effort, accordingly the support also came on its own.

I did find a pattern in my previous association with such insights about mountaineering and the human soul, but this one incident struck the chord or watered the dormant seed of a new adventure within me.

The best gift a parent can give to his or her children is inspiration. Hard work and discipline in studies and other activities of life will come naturally to an inspired child. The investment of time in storytelling to children can bring maximum returns not only to child, but to all humanity. Remember, Alexander was inspired by stories told to him by his mentor, about the richness of India and how one could see the two ends of the world if one stands on mountains of Hindu Kush, in present day Afghanistan.

The same goes for organizations, which inspires their people through their vision and values. Such organizations do not need to create an intricate accountability matrix for their employees. They values of ownership and responsibility comes naturally. Such organizations create a culture for people and society as a whole, to grow and flourish. Inspiration is transformational and not transactional. It stimulates one from within. The results are permanent and sustainable. People, as such, love their profession and place of work, and are self-driven.

What is not inspiration?

I have always been against the concept of motivational talks. Motivation always lies within. No one can motivate another person. If someone does not want money, fame, or any other reward, and finds futile, he cannot be motivated by providing the same. The absence of need or fire within, hinders any kind of motivation. However, inspiration is giving a spark to the latent or dormant need or aspiration. It is the process of giving life. An engine with gasoline does not run till the moment the 'spark' or 'ignition' is turned on. It is the act of striking the right chords in a person to produce to right chords. The music is always there in the instrument but it takes a well-practiced musician to strike the right chord to generate the melody in music.

An inspired being can never go into depression or dejection. His source of inspiration is like a life jacket for him, which keeps him afloat in moments of setbacks and storms. Failures improve an inspired person. No setback really discourages an inspired person.

> "The most powerful weapon on earth is the human soul on fire." -- Ferdinand Foch, military strategist

When to get inspired?

We all know that to live a pleasant and productive life, we need ninety nine percent perspiration and one percent inspiration. But the problem with most of the people is that even this one percent inspiration is missing. The process of inspiration is not one time, but a dynamic one where we need to remember and relive our inspiration every day.

If one sees an inspirational movie or listens to an inspirational talk, but goes back to his routine life in the same environment of mediocrity, then the effect of inspiration fades away soon. To etch it permanently onto our mind and heart, we need to be exposed to our source of inspiration every day and all the time. The process of interaction and communication with our inspiration has to be continuous and consistent. The stimulation has to be long enough to bring permanent changes in us.

Power of Inspiration

An inspired mind can change the way mankind thinks forever. Its immense power can bring long-lasting restructuring and reorganization of the world. The inspired mind is not deterred by the results, for him his work is his journey and every step is worth enjoyment.

The Wright Brothers came from a humble background but their innocent inspiration from the idea of flying set them on a worthy, well-meaning and well-intentioned journey. Lack of resources and their tender ages did not stop them to work on their passion. Even their father told them, 'if God wanted humans to fly, then he would have given him wings'. But inspiration itself is a message from God and true inspiration does not need to be tested against the logic of the day. Due to their incessant trials and errors with deep study and analysis, they discovered the principles of aerodynamics and for the first time in history, a man was flying in a heavier than air object, on chilly morning of 29 Dec 1903. There are no limitations to the journey of an inspired mind.

Inspiration can be of any shape or size but it does play an important role in our life. Without it, we are just like dead men walking and living one day at a time, with no real reason or relevance to live for.

After World War II, thousands of German soldiers, were made to toil and suffer in Russian 'gulags', a term for Russian POW camps, situated in far-away Siberian cold deserts near the Bering Strait. Among so many escape and evasion stories, the saga of Cornelius Rost's nine thousand mile journey home stands out as an astounding achievement of endurance and fortitude. All standards of survival and toil were surpassed. He walked on foot for thousands of kilometers through snow, endured most inclement weather, meandered through most rugged terrains and dealt with hostile people. What kept him going? The intense inspiration and desire to be with his family.

> "If your actions inspire others to dream more, learn more, do more and become more, you are a leader."
> -- John Quincy Adams, 6th President of the United States

The journey of life is about moving from 'where we are' to 'where we want to be'. Our inspiration gives the reason and purpose to move on our journey. As such, it is critical to provide the power or traction for our movement.

"Motivation is everything. You can do the work of two people, but you can't be two people. Instead, you have to inspire the next guy down the line and get him to inspire his people."

-- Lee Iacocca, Auto Executive

4

Define your Vision

"Create the highest, grandest vision possible for your life, because you become what you believe"

-- Oprah Winfrey, Talk Show Host

One cannot work on goals for long before losing one's excitement and energy, if they do not flow from his vision or are not ingrained in his purpose. Most of the time, we do not feel any sense of achievement even after successfully achieving our goals. At times, even success in our life brings us a sense of worthlessness. We feel that something is not right or something is missing and amiss. This is the time to define your vision.

What is a vision?

Of all the living beings on earth, human beings are uniquely capable of setting visions for self. We have been endowed with the awareness of our existence, and uniquely we can decide the reason behind our existence. We can decide what we want to do with ourselves and what should be the terms and tasks on which we want to spend our life. Our instincts are stretched beyond survival. We want to shine and stand-out. Rather than just exist, a human being is born to flourish. We can dream. An animal cannot set dreams for its future but a human being will not survive, if he is devoid of his dreams.

Vision is the ability to see beyond, in the distant future, a state we want to achieve. It is our capability through which we decide 'what we want to be', 'where we want to be', 'how we are to be known' and above all, 'why we exist'. It should be the basic reason for our existence and rudder for our evolution. It is the cause which we love to live and die for. The vision defines and directs us. It is our true identity.

Our vision propels us in the right direction and decides our goals. When goals flow from our vision, we never feel

> Vision is the art of seeing the invisible.
> Jonathan Swift

exhausted in their pursuit. It is like the first button in the shirt, if put correctly then rest of the buttons will fall in place on their own. If it is put incorrectly then rest of the buttons will be out of place. If one finds, defines and lives his vision, he is always inspiring and, initiating action from people.

It is appropriate to say that man make dreams but more importantly, dream makes a man. History is made by dreamers. Whatever we see

> "We are limited not by our abilities but by our vision."
> -- Anonymous

around us, small or big, is a result of someone's vision. It is the foundation of all human endeavors and development.

Dr. Victor Frankl, in his famous book, 'Man's Search for Meaning', aptly describes man as a 'future being'. We always live and love to think and work for the future. If we do find a purpose in our existence, we cease to live. It is sad to see the anti-leadership behavior of present generation when they speak about living for today and not caring for tomorrow. Life is essentially a journey from 'where we are' to 'where we want to be', or more aptly 'what we are' to 'what we want to become'. Living in immediacy is against human natural being, and breeds and brings mediocrity. It does not drive us to action. Whereas as a vision for tomorrow sets us in motion for massive action.

Why do we need a vision?

It is the statement which defines the prime motive of our existence. It is the ground on which our goals and objectives grows. Without a firm ground of vision, the goals soon wither away.

Our goals and objectives flow from our vision. All our decisions and actions are a postlude to it. It is the agency which provides our answers and clarifies our doubts. It gives us a direction in time and space. It is the source of discipline and delayed gratification in one's life, the true ingredients for long term accomplishments and achievements in one's life. Many people start great endeavors on their journey of life, but soon lose interest, and are not able to maintain the discipline of diligent and dedicated effort. They do have goals and objectives but lack vision. They do not find a

> "Vision without action is a daydream. Action without vision is a nightmare."
> -- Japanese Proverb

reason to toil and trudge themselves in pursuit of the set goals. Their goals do not come from a firm well-grounded vision. Ability to delay gratification has been a key quality of all great achievers, and is necessarily a function of a grand vision. A vision for which we are able to sacrifice everything today so that we can gain multiple rewards and contentment of living our vision.

Every organization has a well-defined vision statement which provides the reason for its existence. We never join an organization which does not have a vision, then why do we live in our personal lives without a vision. How can we even align with an organizational vision without having a personal vision? Even marriages fail when people joining in, do not have their own individual visions. A partner needs to be clear in oneself as to what he or she wants out of life and the institution of marriage. Otherwise, it leads to confusion and chaos, even when no one is at fault.

When our vision does not match with that of our organization or partner, or our environment does not support it, we feel frustration and suffocation. We start sensing 'something is not right'. We start facing the slow death of our soul. Our true identity gets lost. We cease to grow and develop.

Leadership and vision

As a leadership trainer (and student), I have always found vision at the core of any leader. In fact, I would say, vision is

> Leadership is the capacity to translate vision into reality.
> -Warren Bennis

the identity of a leader. No vision, no leader. Leadership process is initiated with the realization of a vision. During my trainings I never speak about leadership qualities before elucidating the indispensability of a vision for a leader. The leadership qualities will subsequently develop by trial and errors. Like any other skill, it can be developed in the pursuit of one's vision. Leadership is not just discovering or deciphering one's own vision but stimulating and inspiring others to do the same.

The essence of leadership is to sacrifice for, and surrender to, a vision. The work may look very small but if it is entrenched in a vision, a person will not only rise soon but will relish his work. It is not humble beginnings but the direction which should be the source of all motivation for long-term sustained efforts. A destination or landmark on our journey may have its limitations in terms of relevance and results and we may get bored with it but the right direction is timeless and true motivation.

Human spirit and vision

As per ancient scriptures, we all are born with a pre-defined purpose and play our individual roles. As humans, we need to discover and deliver them. If we are born as human, we need to justify this and live according to our natural design.

A honey bee has around six thousand neurons in her brain, and she works and justifies her existence by making her beehive, mating, reproducing, collecting nectar and dying. As human beings, we have ninety five to one hundred twenty five billion neurons in our brain, but what do we do? Grow up, get a job, earn money, build a house, have children and die. If we are designed differently from honey bees there has to be a reason behind. We are supposed to live differently. In fact, scientifically it has been proved that the human brain is far bigger than the one required to run the basic functions of human body, unlike in any other animal. We need to realize that a human brain is designed for some purpose to be achieved, problem to solved and produce something worthwhile.

I feel sad, when I see the sole aim of a student in our schools is to clear a competitive exam, get admission in a good college and subsequently get a high paying job. Education should not aim at merely earning a livelihood, but to liberate oneself from the shackles of ignorance. It should

> The future belongs to those who see possibilities before they become obvious.
> John Scully

inculcate a higher self-awareness and finding one's purpose and vision. It should aim at unlocking the human potential, and help him to gain a wide perspective of life where he can appreciate and accommodate different ideas and ideologies. Also, getting good grades should not be related to answering mediocre questions, but the ability to ask difficult, different and daring questions.

For any country to grow and develop, the environment to let people envision and endure should be the sole responsibility of its governance. That is the

> A city is not gauged by its length and width, but by the broadness of its vision and the height of its dreams.
> -Herb Caen

only way to harness and hone the talent of a nation and develop a country. The purpose of all education should be to inculcate the habit of grand envisioning and leading self and others to its realization.

Where can one find his vision? Within or with-out?

I feel it is both, one finds his true vision where his inside world connects with outside world. Like inspiration, this too cannot be bought or borrowed. It has to be discovered and defined. One should fully own and be emotional about his vision. Only right emotions set you in motion.

For this one needs to relate and release himself to the outside world. It is a time taking conscious process and needs divine providence. If we keep running and do not stop to think, then how can we make mid-course corrections? We need to break from our busy schedules and must find time to think. Today being busy has become the parameter of

> Your vision will become clear only when you can look into your own heart. Who looks outside, dreams; who looks inside, awakes.
> -Carl Jung

success. However, I find it more a failure than a success. A rat keeps running throughout his life but does not reach anywhere. He keeps himself busy, but to no avail. Busy-ness does not ensure greatness. It is the journey in right direction which makes us grow to greatness. Do not make conscious efforts to search for a vision. Just flow effortlessly with the world, and observe and connect to the nature and world around us, to arrive at your vision.

What does vision give?

Vision gives us a sense of direction and destination. It aligns us, most importantly with ourselves. In my military training, I had a deep interest in navigation exercises, where one has to find one's present location, then the direction and distance to the given destination and then move to this destination without any track or trail to guide. The suitable path had to be determined and the principles of navigation had to be applied. I am thankful to the Army for teaching me leadership through this simple exercise. I realized that to reach any destination we need four things:

1. Present Location (Point A). If we do not know where we stand today, then even if we know the destination, we cannot chalk out a route.
2. Proposed Destination (Point B). A pre-determined destination is essential. If we do not know where we have to go, then it does not matter which route we take.
3. Path. There could be a myriad number of possible paths to reach from Point A to Point B. But the skill lies in finding the most suitable path, in which we utilize our minimum resources viz. time, efforts, men, material and so on. The shortest path may not always be the most suitable path.

4. Principles. The universe is dictated by a number of natural principles which cannot denied. We need to abide by them and use them to our advantage.

With the knowledge of principles of navigation, and belief in the timeless tools of magnetic compass and maps, we were able to navigate through tortuous terrain, under inclement weather, successfully to our destination. The key was not to lose track of direction (degrees) and distance (steps). Nothing else mattered.

It is applicable in every sphere of life. As long as we stick to the direction provided by our vision and follow the natural principles that guide us, we will navigate successfully and reach our destination.

Let us say, a person wants to reduce weight and stay healthy. First he needs to find out his present weight before even deciding the weight he wants to achieve. Point A is more important than Point B. Only

> "Give us clear vision that we may know where to stand and what to stand for- because unless we stand for something we shall fall for anything"
> -Peter Marshall

then he can find how much weight he has to reduce (or even may have to gain). After that he has to decide the method or path, while considering the principles of human metabolism and biology, depending on his suitability and requirements. He may go for crash dieting for faster results, or yoga for slower and sustainable results.

What makes a good vision?

Vision needs to be moral, ethical and above all, transformational. It should create a story of inspiration for generations to come. It must bring some positive change in and for the society. It should truly illustrate the saying, 'how the world is a better place because I lived here'.

Once a young man, named Joe, goes to a library and borrows a thick book. After reading for a long time, he goes to the librarian and asks, what kind of book is it, there are so many characters but no story in making. The librarian replies, that the book is a telephone directory. This simple and short joke illustrates one important aspect of human psyche by virtue of which every human being likes to be a privy or part of a story. We do not like meaningless and or message-less things. We like STORIES.

Who and what creates stories. In any story, we know through movies, books or story-telling, few things are common, a chaos, crisis, confusion or calamity; a person takes charge to change; and through his courageous struggle to overcome the disorder and bringing a new order. The 'hero' faces many setbacks, and stumbles many a time, but the movie ends only when his work is over.

No book is written or movie is made about mediocrity. We all like to see the endurance in the search and struggle for excellence. That is how a human being is. As such, we

> You've got to think about big things while you're doing small things, so that all the small things go in the right direction.
> Alvin Toffler

need to move on our journey in a way that we feel it can create a story for people to remember and relive.

Great Visions

Great vision can take birth at any time without our conscious thinking or effort. It is just the inner voice which is heard for very short and shaky bursts. One needs great care and concentration to listen to it. It may occur in times of solitude, like General Arjun Ray envisioning the establishment of a new concept of education, while sitting on the banks of river Indus in Ladakh. Or it may occur in extreme situations which jolts a person to the core and instigate him to question his sole existence, like Mahatama Gandhi who was pushed out of a compartment of a train meant only for 'whites'. This one incident gave him a purpose and vision to fight for equality, through non-violence. It was a major breakthrough in the tools and tactics of war and brought a revolution. This vision for equality was even bigger than the goal of Indian independence.

Visionaries are behind every projection and progression of mankind in different fields and forays. A grand vision always summons the deepest desire, drudgery, demands and daring from humans.

Thomas Alva Edison invented the modern electric bulb in nineteen century and

> The empires of the future are empires of the mind.
> Winston Churchill

established an electric grid to power it. The innovation not only diffused the boundaries between day and night, but gave a whole new comfort and environment to mankind. Stephen Hawking's work on astrophysics not only diffused the boundaries between science and religion but questioned the purpose of not only our existence but the existence and evolution of whole universe. John F Kennedy's call to his nation to put the man on moon and bring him back safely, demanded a whole new imagination and innovation from the realms of science and scientists, and changed the dimensions of human exploration forever. Under John Hunt's able leadership and through great camaraderie of the team, Edmund Hillary and Tenzing Norgay stepped on the apex of earth, Mount Everest, on 29 May, 1953. The incident set new standards of excellence and desire to endure and exist in the place where humans are not meant to be present, for all generations to come.

Defining and deciding a vision is a phase of journey

Defining and deciding a vision is a time-taking process and not a one-time affair. It is not a milestone but a phase of our journey, where great deal of dissonance and resonance happens within us and around us. We come to know how we are required by this world or the universe at large.

Working towards a grand vision, whether ours' or anyone else's provides us with an internal bliss and is innate to human race. It energizes us to massive action, and provides us with a meaningful living. By their very nature, humans either develop their own vision or get attracted to someone else's vision. We like to associate with a vision in which we find some resonating emotional cause, and we can see our efforts contributing to the big picture. With a leadership perspective, it is essential to generate an emotional connect among people towards a vision and show how each individual effort will contribute to the larger cause.

I remember when I used to work in a bank, I had a great boss and good remuneration, but something was missing. Performance bonuses were

> It is not the logic or reasoning but the emotions behind an endeavor which motivates us.
> -Mohit Tomar

lucrative, performance parameters were lucid but were not able to generate the right emotions within me. I was not able to find a cause or reason to be passionate about. Of course, banks are indispensable to economic growth and financial well-being of a country but I was not able to connect with this concept. Deep introspection and intervention within me led me to move into training, and live my cause of enabling people to live more productive and pleasant lives through my leadership training. My reflections led me to conclude that we need to connect to a vision emotionally and see our contribution to a bigger cause.

If we are not able to define or decide our own vision at present, it is advisable to associate with people or organizations with a grand vision. We just need to work towards a great vision, no matter in what capacity, to lead a happy life. A great life is the pursuit of a great vision. It keeps us excited, energized and enthusiastic.

No matter how small or big, a worthwhile vision is an asset on any journey of human life. It provides us the impetus and impulse to move on effortlessly and with efforts without getting tired and trodden.

"We act as though comfort and luxury were the chief requirements of life, when all that we need to make us really happy is something to be enthusiastic about."

-- Charles Kingsley, clergyman

5

Decide your Values

"Here is your country. Cherish these natural wonders, cherish the natural resources, cherish the history and romance as a sacred heritage, for your children and your children's children. Do not let selfish men or greedy interests skin your country of its beauty, its riches or its romance."

— Theodore Roosevelt

Human's biggest dilemma in life is to find 'what is right' and 'what is wrong'. Even after years full of varied experience, we are not able to find a convincing answer, at times, to these simple questions. It is the biggest source of confusion and chaos in our lives, and diminishes and dulls our decision making capability. Life is grey and poses us a challenge to sift through various vague and blurred options. The journey through this muddled and cluttered road of life requires clarity within oneself, as things outside are disarrayed and diffused. The challenge is always to find clarity out of this ambiguity. But how shall we do it.

We need to have values.

The word 'value has a wide range of meanings in different domains. In our present context it means "degree to which something is useful or estimable". In simple words, it means what one values over other things in life. It is a set of guidelines or parameters which ones sets, to decide the

> "How can one be well... when one suffers morally?"
> — Leo Tolstoy, War and Peace

means to achieve one's ends. It is like a compass or GPS for a navigator, which helps to make midcourse corrections and bring us back on track. A person who is firmly grounded in the right values cannot take actions for which he will have to repent later, physically, emotionally or most importantly, morally. If vision gives us a destination, values decides the course of action.

What are the right values?

The sole purpose of all our religious studies, contemporary education and organizational training is to inculcate right values, which will help us to produce long term and lasting results benefiting everyone and nature as well. There are certain values which are timeless, self-evident and universal in bringing universal peace and prosperity. Integrity, respect, care, love, discipline, hard work, empathy, honesty, loyalty, and so on. These are some of the good values a person or culture can incorporate in its ethics or ethos.

Two of these values needs a special mention and elaboration, as they covers most of the other values.

- **Integrity.**
  It is the most widely used term whenever the subject of values is discussed. It is different from honesty or loyalty, but provides them as its corollary. As per the dictionary, it means 'the state of being whole, entire or undiminished'. A person with integrity is whole and complete in himself, when his physical, mental, emotional and spiritual aspects become one. He

achieves singularity and is at peace with self. His thoughts, words and actions are in sync without any dilemma and doubts. He has nothing to hide or risk. He is in perfect balance or equation with the outer world or his environment.

• **Empathy**

All the world's disturbances, difference and distances will be removed if we look at the world by getting into others' shoes. The rifts and rivalries between people, cultures and countries can be removed if we start understanding the other's perspectives. As humans, we all have individual and unique thinking and targets in life, so it is a big challenge for us to understand each other. Animals do not have such a challenge and live in peace with each other with mutual respect, care and love. They follow strict discipline on social and survival platforms. But as humans we need to look for a better and bigger context to overcome these individual differences. Ironically, we are not so different; as all of us want love, empathy, respect, recognition and care, as the end result and reason for our lives. Our ways of understanding and expression may be different but at the core, our requirements and urges are all same.

Why do we require right values?

We have a choice of actions to achieve our goals. There may be options which save our resources but may still bring exhaustion and guilt for us. On

"It's not hard to make decisions when you know what your values are."
— Roy Disney

the other hand, a few options may be more tiring, tortuous and twisted, but in the end give us peace of mind and a high sense of self-respect. One test I always recommend is for everyone who seek to decide their vision and values. If we can exemplify our vision and values in front of our children, with pride and dignity, and see them emulating the same, then we are on the right track. Also, if we can face ourselves in the mirror, while looking at ourselves straight in the eyes and feel a high sense of self-pride and self-respect, then we should move on with it.

The right values are a manifestation of nature. The world around us is the best teacher to teach these. For example, if we see the ecosystem in forests, the perfect balance of everything is clearly visible. Everything is in harmony with the other. Removal of any aspect or entity may lead to the crumbling of the entire system. Everyone grows to their fullest potential without harming the other. In fact, every entity plays a crucial role in the perseverance and perpetuation of the entire ecosystem.

The interconnectedness and interdependence of the entire human civilization cannot be denied. This continuity in human community has to be sustained and strengthened, and we need to respect and recognize the needs of each other so as to lift the others up so as to uplift ourselves. In any system, everyone grows together. No one grows in isolation. A person well-connected is far more happy and fulfilled than those who live in isolation. Even countries grow together viz. the nations of the Far East; Australia and New Zealand, and Europe. On the other hand, where neighboring countries have been fighting for decades, not only the expenses have sapped the countries of their resources, the chaos did not let people to engage in productive endeavors, and their overall wellbeing has been imbalanced.

The right values are the ones which keeps us in sync with everyone else and our complete environment. It not only lets us grow to our fullest, to realize our full potential and mature into what we are meant to be, but also brings out the growth and development of our environment along with ours. We need to think of humanity as one large organism, with each of us as one of its more than six billion cells, just as we are each an organism made of thirty seven trillion cells. If a few cells face a problem, then the complete organism suffers.

How can we develop a prosperous and peaceful culture?

The simple belief, "Do unto others as you want them to do unto you" summarizes the entire dynamics of treating

> Wrong intentions cannot bring right outcomes.
> -Mohit Tomar

people and environment around us. If we want our society and nature to take care of us, we need to take care of it. If we want respect, we need to give respect. If we want love, we need to give love. And so on.

How do we develop values?

Consciously or unconsciously, we all develop certain norms and standards on which we assess things and take decisions. These depends on the environment, society, culture or country we grow in; or how we reflect on our experiences.

- Role modeling
  Like our ancestors in the evolution tree, we are good at imitation, through which not only do we learn basic skills of living but also understand how to conform to the practices and norms of environment and society. Our intentions and actions are always judged against the values practiced in the society we live in. Our society, which essentially consists of our friends, family and associates is the key to our values. Any philosophy or practice we see as being productive in our immediate environment is readily accepted as a value. It may be wrong or harmful in the long run, but we do what we see others doing. As such, as we need to model the right practices in a proactive manner.

  For imbibing any kind of value, age is a crucial factor. Most of our personality, in terms of our belief system, is complete by the time we turn five, which is our most formative period. As such, it is imperative to be a right role model to our young ones. It is our responsibility to restructure the future of our culture through right upbringing of our future generation.

- Leadership

  Leadership at different levels plays a pivotal role in rolling out standards for society. Today, we are facing a leadership lacuna in our society, and filling this gap is the requirement of the day. Incidents such as a teacher not being on time to class, a local police officer crossing a red light at traffic signal, or a minister taking a bribe are equally grave and have equal impact in determining and displaying the value system of a culture. Sadly, in our country the intellectual and cognitive assimilation are the prime criteria for critical leadership roles in different fields, with no heed paid to one's vision and values. We respect people on the basis of the position they hold rather than the ingenuity of their thoughts and actions, which could bring peace and prosperity to society.

  Leaders in any capacity have a very critical role, of deciding and conveying the right values for themselves and his team. As such, leadership is not a privilege but a burden. This burden has to be carried with utmost responsibility and accountability. Since leadership is a 'future department' of a group or 'future faculty' of an individual, as such, each small or big act of his will decide the future of the group or himself.

Right values are critical to the sustenance of societies

Our value system is expressed through our actions and not through words. We are living and displaying our values, at

> The first step in the evolution of ethics is a sense of solidarity with other human beings.
> - Albert Schweitzer

every moment. It is the most economical and effective way of our branding and marketing. Today, we gauge people, organizations, societies and even countries on the basis of how they live. The harmony within their society and their contributions to humanity at large, mirrors their right values and righteous existence.

One small incident I experienced in Singapore is etched in mind forever. When I landed at Changi Airport and inquired of a local man the bus route to my hotel, he not only guided me but also asked me "Sir, Do you have change?" When I asked why, he explained that the bus driver may not be able accept a large currency note. He the exchanged coins with me. This empathy and care was a small but impactful episode, of the friendly and empathetic culture of the country.

Following right values may give us temporary trouble and provisional pain but the results are long lasting and we live a life of harmony and happiness. Wrong values such as greed,

> "Always do what is right. It will gratify half of mankind and astound the other."
> — Mark Twain

hate, unfairness, illegitimate gains, dishonesty and such, may give us short term gains but will de-stabilize the whole eco-system in a short time and the results will reflect on us.

The recent financial turmoil and troubles the world went through is a direct consequence of wrong values. The financial meltdown of the year 2008 was a natural consequence of the unethical and amoral behavior of few people who were driven by personal greed. It is no surprise that the gravity of the subject of ethics in business studies, has been realized and emphasized in leading business schools.

One name which comes to my mind when I speak of ethics and ethos, is Colonel Sathya Rao, my mentor and Director at the Indus School of Leadership. The best lesson I got from him is the value of 'being a good human'. He exhibits the utmost level of integrity in nurturing talent and transforming lives of his team. His goodness is infectious and people follow him voluntarily, as he carries an aura of integrity and respect around him. His care and concern for each individual in the entire organization, creates an environment which is conducive for overall growth and progress. No surprise that today 'being a good human' summarizes all management, military and other training.

The Alexander the Great, recognized and revered as the world's most renowned conqueror, controlled a far smaller territory than that of Genghis Khan, at the height of his power. Still he is addressed as the Greatest of All and has been a source of inspiration and stimulus for generations like an immortal. Why? His compassion, chivalry and charm was infectious and enabled him to win hearts and minds of people throughout the world even in the territories beyond his kingdom and time far beyond into future. If his military genius and strong leadership facilitated his conquests; his attitude towards people, friends and enemies, men and women, deep rooted in right values, helped him to attain peace and prosperity thereafter.

> Great people have great values and great ethics.
> -Jeffrey Gitomer

One day, I was watching a documentary on the construction of Marina Bay Sands on the National Geographic channel, and was mesmerized with the creativity and courage that had gone into building that iconic structure, defying the previous norms of architectural engineering. The aspect which gripped me was the amount of wisdom and work they had to put into making a firm foundation for the structure to stand on. It was not possible for the huge weight of concrete to stand firmly on the soft black mud on the reclaimed land in sea. As such, the team had to spend a good deal of time, effort and money to generate a novel solution to address this problem and make a stable base for the building to stand on. I learnt the lesson that for any beautiful structure to stand, a firm foundation is a pre-requisite. Although most of the time this is not visible or felt, but any big success is made up of the right values, lived day in and day out.

No doubt, Mercedes Benz, known for its super-efficient and safe cars, lived their values by recalling thousands of cars, due to some minor snag. This gesture reinforced their vision and values of being number one in quality. It truly exemplified their belief in caring for their customers. When the Indian cricketer, Sachin Tendulkar turned down the offer to endorse a liquor brand, he lived his value of caring for the health of his countrymen.

Discovering right values

With regard to discovering the right values, our own judgement and conscience supersedes all. Whenever we face a dilemma in the journey of life, about what is wrong or right, we just need to look deep within us into our conscience and ask basic questions. To identify and internalize the right values, we need answer the questions such as 'What do I stand for?', 'What agitates me?', 'What wrong doing does not follow my conscience?', 'What course of action brings me peace of mind?', 'Do my actions harm my people or my ecosystem?', 'How will my action contribute to the overall good?', 'Will my choice fall back on me in a negative manner?', and so on.

Every country has a constitution from which its decisions and laws flow. Every organization has clearly defined values. But do we have the same for ourselves? I would even recommend having well-written values for selves and our families. Whenever there is a crisis or confusion, we know where to find the answers and actionable(s). When an organization is hiring employees or a person is choosing his life partner, it makes sense to know the values of the prospective people. Also, we need to check and balance our values with those of our organization.

If we study, there is a direct correlation between the overall health and happiness of a country and the way animals are treated, women

> Live one day at a time emphasizing ethics rather than rules.
> -Wayne Dyer

are respected, children are taken care of, and even prisoners are shown empathy. Even the best business deals are the ones where everyone wins and grows. The right values bring overall good. I take pride in belonging to this country, where the most evolved culture existed at one time. It is in this country that kings retired and moved on in search for higher goals and completing their journey of life successfully. When too much gold came to this country in exchange for spices, the king sent his emissaries to those countries to ensure that their resources were not depleted and a long-term relations of friendship and trade could be ensured.

When England was in bad shape during World War II, the Prime Minister, Winston Churchill was asked about the future of the country and the necessary course of action. He just asked one question, "Is justice being done in our courts and are people taken care of in our country?" When he received the answer 'Yes', he conveyed, "Then nothing bad will happen to this country". So insightful and true.

Here I need to clarify that manners and etiquette are not necessarily right values. They are just gestures and are relative to a culture. They have no meaning or significance if they do not arise from the emotions of true caring, respect and love at the core of person. A well-mannered person may not have right values. Manners denotes the grooming of a person but values lie at the core of a person and his spiritual and emotional evolution.

Not following the right values may put ourselves at odds with our environment. By following a path of the right values, our journey becomes our goal. Every step taken on this path is in itself an achievement and brings us a sense of accomplishment. Our journey should bring overall and lasting benefits and health.

"The best morals kids get from any book is just the capacity to empathize with other people, to care about the characters and their feelings. So you don't have to write a preachy book to do that. You just have to make it a fun book with characters they care about, and they will become better people as a result."

— Louis Sachar

6

Be with Right People

My idea of good company is the company of clever, well-informed people who have a great deal of conversation; that is what I call good company.

Jane Austen

6

Be with Right People

My idea of good company is the company of clever, well-informed people who have a great deal of conversation; that is what I call good company.

Jane Austen

The journey of life is quite an individual and ingenious enterprise. But like great projects which cannot be accomplished by an individual, great journeys transcend the individual, and affect and gets affected positively by fellow human beings. Great journeys are achieved through great associations.

A great deal of resources are spent by organizations in every domain, to get the right people on board. Even choosing friends and life partners is a challenge. The present competitive scenario poses no dearth of talented and skilled people. At the click of a few buttons we can access huge data of people with degrees from leading institutions and work experience from elite organizations. There is no dearth of talent, skills and other credentials. But the challenge is getting the right people.

Who are the right people?

If we refer to a dictionary, the word 'right' means to be 'in accordance with what is good, proper, or just' and also to be 'in conformity with fact, reason, truth, or some standard or principle; correct'. As such, we can deduce it to be an absolute entity and also context specific.

Does it depend on the task? A task or a piece of work can be accomplished through the right skill hired at a competitive price. But to move on a journey, a journey of life, a journey with a great vision, it needs right people and not just right skills. The journey of life surpasses and outshines the

> "Don't become pigeonholed into thinking the person with the exact necessary experience is the right person for the role," said Tom Gimbel, CEO and founder of staffing and recruiting firm LaSalle Network.

work or job we do to earn a livelihood. It is about creating an identity of ourselves through self-exploration. As such, to know the right people, we need to have a larger perspective of what is life's journey and what kind of people will make a positive impact on it. How can different journeys coalesce into one big movement? How can the talents and tasks can be matched and meaning be derived.

An organization needs right people and not just right 'talent' or 'skill' to excel and evolve. A society needs right people who can transform it to a higher order of living. A person needs the right life partner to know himself better and grow to his fullest potential. Even to know oneself and metamorphose to fully express oneself, one needs to be 'right'.

I always believe in the power of fundamentals and basics. If they are in place, the bigger picture will take care of itself. A person who follows the path of 'righteousness', will be able enjoy the journey of life, while fulfilling his duties and responsibilities enroute. Then the person transcends the boundaries of roles and responsibilities. At that stage, change and contribution becomes his way of expression. He grows from routine to re-evolution.

I do agree that every organization society or family has a certain set of ethos and ethics which underpins its beliefs, traditions and customs. As such, the right choice of people is crucial for the sustenance of the system. We are all different but still very much the same. We all have different ways of expressing ourselves but we all want to express the same basic human needs. We all have different languages, but we express the same emotions. We all have different practices but want to produce the same things. We worship in different ways or may not worship at all, but all of us ultimately recognize some divine power. We all want love, respect, empathy and recognition regardless of our backgrounds. God made all of us 'right', he never does 'rough work'. We all have innate potential and talent. But this 'being right' needs to be nurtured and nourished in the right context. If a person is living on a path of righteousness, he can adapt to and accommodate himself to any environment and flourish in it. He can fit into any context.

Education should aim not only at delivering subject knowledge and skills but also should aim at teaching 'being right' at the core of the curriculum. The

> "It is the nature of man to rise to greatness if greatness is expected of him."
> -- John Steinbeck, author

students need to be taught and trained to be in relevance and relationship with the environment and time. Adaptability and flexibility are the keys to change management and ultimate growth and development.

Also, being right is living as per the natural principles of life and following an ethical and moral code of conduct. Without righteousness, no knowledge can lead us on a worthwhile path. In fact an educated immoral person is a bigger threat to the society than an uneducated immoral person. 'Righteousness' is a universal and timeless virtue and brings peace and prosperity for all. This is the most permanent education and imperative to the sustenance of mankind.

What makes a person right?

We grow to our fullest potential in the right environment which stretches us beyond our limits and also supports in the process. It challenges us and cares for us. Similarly, the right person is one with whom we grow. The association which we belong to decide our future and wellbeing. The right people provide us with the right environment for us in which we bloom.

1. **Optimism.**
   The flow of positive energy is central to all great lives and achievement. We attract prosperity through positivity. It propels us to action and persistence in times of setbacks. A positive mind always focuses on the goal and sees opportunity in failures. We need to keep positive people around us, who encourage and cheer us on.

2. **Support**

    Great works are not accomplished alone. We all need support of other human beings for us to grow. Choose tenacious people whom you can rely on in times of adversity and crisis. Such people are few but those few are enough for this world to go around.

3. **Connect**

    Most of the time, people are not wrong. They just do not fit into the jigsaw of our lives. We need people who just connect to us, emotionally and mentally and above all, spiritually. The biggest asset a person can have is people who can understand him, who can plug into his emotions and think at the same intellectual level. Most importantly, we need to have people who believe in our purpose and support what we stand for.

4. **Stretch**

    This is the most important quality of people we need to have around us. Any living being blooms when it is stretched outside its comfort zone. If people around us always agree with us, then we are surely doomed in the near future. We need people who challenges the status quo and sets new standards of excellence.

5. **Value**

    Association with people who are more knowledgeable and experienced than us is crucial for our decision making and planning. Only one who is enlightened

    > For every one of us that succeeds, it's because there's somebody there to show you the way out.
    > -Oprah Winfrey

himself can bring enlightenment to others. A person is doomed when he does not have access or association with people who can give advice with right values and long-term benefits.

It is not an exaggeration to say that our destiny is dependent on the kinds of people we associate with or relate to.

Recently, saw a woman crying in a court pleading with the judge to solve her matrimonial dispute. After seven long years of battling in court, the case has not been concluded, due to the ill-intended motives of the woman who wanted her husband to suffer because of the women centric laws, by filing false complaints. Rightly, we should not start what we cannot finish. The man opted to fight the case and proved his innocence. The case was made complicated due to bad intentions, wrong judgement and immoral decisions, made under the influence of 'wrong' people around the woman. Otherwise, the issue could have been solved amicably through mutual discussion and decision-making, just like the way in which the marriage took place.

How to choose right people?

If there is one talent which comes first in moving successfully on the journey of life, then it is the ability to ascertain and assess the right people we find en route. We need to have the right companion to make it more exciting and enriching.

I realized, while running a cross country race that it is boring and discouraging to run alone. Finally, when I started matching my pace with one of my team mates, the run became less tiring. Thereafter, we both encouraged and stretched each other beyond our limits of performance. However, it is important to choose the right mate, in terms of speed and connect. The speed of the mate should not be too slow or too fast for you. It must create the stretch and challenge for you to perform at a higher level. Also, the emotional and mental connect makes all the difference. With some people, we just do not feel right.

It is sad to see that in today's world, when I see too much focus on degrees, certificates and other such tangible credentials. They may give some indication about how the person may have lived his life but they do guarantee integrity, trust, loyalty, adaptability, tenacity and collaboration from the person chosen. Even when choosing a life partner, in our Indian society, the degree and job profile makes the prime criteria for selection. But what about the character and characteristics of the person. We need to focus on the basic questions like who are his friends and other people in his circle, where does he spend his time, what does he like to search on the net, what kinds of books does he read, what kinds of movies he watch, and so on, to get a more vivid and real picture of him.

> There is a saying that every nice piece of work needs the right person in the right place at the right time.
> -Benoit Mandelbrot

If one wants to know a person, just get to know the people he likes to be with. What or who we are decides whom we want to be with and also whom we are with decides who we are. 'Birds of a feather, flock together'. We are our thoughts, which in turn is reflected in our daily living. So to know a person, just see how he lives.

Essentially we do not even need to choose the right people. They just gravitate towards us. We need to be original and cautious in what we convey to outside world, and we convey what we are, not what we say or do. It is about the invisible chemistry of right bonding and also the physics of like attracting like. If one feels positive one will attract positive people. If one is ambitious, one will attract ambitious people. If a person has high integrity, he will attract people with integrity. If a man likes adventure, he

> It sounds like a cliche but I also learnt that you're not going to fall for the right person until you really love yourself and feel good about how you are.
> -Emma Watson

will attract adventurous people. As such, it all starts from within. We are what we think, which in turn creates our environment in terms of people and resources.

My friends have played a very vital role in my life and my journey of life could not have been same without their support and care. I did not make any deliberate efforts to find them. It just happened with the natural flow of my life. Like attracts like.

The difference between human and other living beings is that we can create our environment, whereas others are the results of their environment. We are the only creatures on earth who are endowed with the power of awareness and proactive decision and action. As such, we need to take care regarding whom we sit with, speak and share our life with in terms of friends, life partner, society or organization. If we miss the calling or purpose in our contribution to an organization, then we should look forward to a new workplace where we enjoy the shared beliefs, values and vision. If we are stuck in a relationship which is restricting the growth of both and the spark of passion and love is missing then we should amicably and affably move out on our individual journeys. If we do not enjoy, entrust, educate and evolve with our friends, then it cannot be defined as friendship.

We should not get confused between being irresponsible and immoral, I do not mean to leave our friends and relationships, if we do not feel good about them. Duties and responsibilities have to be fulfilled. We need to do what we love but also love what we do. We cannot just change the people around us irresponsibly. But we should take care about not spending time with negative and hopeless people, who sap our energy and excitement. Attitude is always infectious and can be dangerous, as it moves at a slow speed which affects us without our detection or discernment. If you feel low on energy and low on motivation, one should change these friends. Detachment is not necessarily physical distancing but the conscious effort of tuning out of a negative environment.

Some people come into our lives for a reason and some for a season. But all do have a purpose, this is the way we are inspired, strengthened, enlightened, stretched, nurtured, cared for, and consoled. Our success and happiness is a product of well-coordinated and well-orchestrated events and people around us. Friendship is not an act of partying together or enjoying life together, but a spiritual experience of growing together. Just like a seed needs external environment of warm soil, water and air to grow; we need the right environment of right people to grow with. It is our interaction with other entities that brings growth and development. Can we imagine a seed kept in a cupboard growing into a plant? Similarly, how can a human being become successful and be happy in isolation.

How does being with right people affect our lives?

Right action at right time produces right results. But most importantly, it is the

> Our goal should be others' growth and independence.

right people which make all the difference. If we are with right people, even our mistakes and miscalculations can be checked and corrected in a timely manner. Even if we deviate towards wrong path, we can be brought back on the right track. In fact a person is as powerful, in terms of knowledge, skills, and wisdom, as the people he knows. If we are friends with one happy person, we can get access to an unlimited number of happy people. If we know a successful person, we can get access to unlimited success. If we are with one right person, we can get infinite access to righteousness…and enjoy the trust, love, empathy and compassion of human relations. Moving on such a journey of life itself is a goal worth achieving.

Friendship is born at that moment when one person says to another: "What? You too? I thought I was the only one."

- C S Lewis

7

Live to Learn

Live as if you were to die tomorrow. Learn as if you were to live forever.

Mahatma Gandhi

Life is a learning. It will be incomplete, if not wrong, to say that we learn to live, because in real sense, we live to learn. In fact all the knowledge the mankind has accumulated is itself the result of lives of people. The sole purpose of life is to learn, it is the ultimate human endeavor and purpose. Anyone who takes birth 'will make a living', but those who learn and grow will actually 'live'. Darwin has lucidly explained the theory of evolution, through the principles of 'natural selection', 'survival of the fittest', and 'adaptability' and so on. The most prominent inference from his work is the criticality of learning for survival. Those who learned new skills and accommodated new environment into their thinking pattern, survived.

Life is not a routine, it is evolution. History is proof of the fact that any person, organization or culture withers away if they adhere to a status quo. The journey of life needs movement and entails some form of dissonance or disturbance. Only an agitated or stimulated mind brings valuable changes to this world. That is why a human being needs inspiration and encouragement.

How do we learn?

To human, learning is as natural as play and enjoyment. It is a pleasant experience to know more, understand more and be more. Every skill and

> Live as if you were to die tomorrow. Learn as if you were to live forever.
> -Mahatma Gandhi

knowledge has a shelf life and needs to be developed upon. Movement is the key. We need to move from the known to what is unknown. All the learning happens outside our comfort zone. Someone has rightly brought this out 'If we keep doing the same things again and again, we will keep getting the same results again and again'.

1. **Explore.**

   Exploration has been the identity of mankind since the beginning of his creation. It is natural for a human to explore different places, people and practices. Whether for economic or political interests, education or tourism, we like to move to other places. We like to make alliances with people from different places. We like to appreciate and accommodate art, science and other practices from other worlds. Even wars are a result of this trait in mankind. When we finished traveling our mother Earth, we set our eyes on other planets and 'aliens'. Exploration of the outside world and also of our inner world 'within', is the key to get better picture of ourselves and our environment, at a local or universal level. Exploration is the key to higher awareness. A journey full of exploration and enquiries can enable us to live a life of learning.

2. **Change.**

   The human being or even the universe as whole, is dynamic, and is changing every moment. The way the universe has been evolving since the big bang, or our earth has grown and changed, is proof that change is truly the most permanent thing. Even our body cells gets replaced completely every two years. Every subject needs new understanding and updating. Every tool, gear or instrument needs re-invention. Today there is much excitement and energy put into creating new versions of software and hardware, but what about our very own 'selves'. Are we putting enough research and re-creation to us, so as to be relevant to the present time and environment? Work on self is the biggest work we can do. We must grow and develop, to adapt to the changing environment.

3. **Challenge**

   Response to challenge is a natural way to grow and develop. A man devoid of all challenges is virtually dead. Only one person does not have challenges to face, the one who is in the grave. Children provide us the clearest picture of our natural programming. Their minds are full of possibilities and they like to explore and enquire about themselves and their world, by exposing themselves to new challenges. They are not afraid of failures and persist in finding new ways of doing things, even in face of failure. A child in initial years takes challenges and setbacks as a natural way of life, whether he is learning to cycle, trying to climb a chair or playing a video game.

4. **Dream**

During my college years, I was repeatedly told to follow a certain proven career path and live a satisfied and settled life. I always felt uncomfortable with the idea of a settled life. How can a life be settled, for a person who is 'living'? Life is not about routine but revolution. We need to evolve again and again. The moment we feel a sort of 'settled' in life, I think it is time to change and move on. If we are satisfied and feel there is nothing much to contribute to our organization, society or our own life, we are virtually dead or retired from life. All developments in terms of inventions and discoveries in science, compositions of music, aesthetics of art, revolution through reforms and so on, have been brought about by people who were not satisfied. They felt a gap in the environment and felt the requirement for change and reinitiating of self.

The journey of life can be completed successfully only when it is full of learning. A worthwhile life is a medley of rich and varied experiences. The vastness and vividness of our experiences defines the size of our lives and the learnings gained in them. Learning and living are indispensable.

Why shall we learn?

Everything we need to learn is dependent on what we want in our lives and most importantly how we connect to the divine. Our birth is not our decision but still it is the best thing that happened to us. In the same way we do decide on our goals and make plans to acquire the resources, skills and knowledge, but there is a divine intervention which ensures our overall welfare and well-being. Tapping into this divine power and wisdom can give us access to unlimited power. The terrain and timings of our journey is beyond the human mind and its reasoning. We need to see the bigger picture and the bigger benefits that God has decided for us. Failures and setbacks are ways to make us better and not bitter. A body builder needs to do resistance training to develop muscles. Of course it will generate lactic acid and temporary discomfort, but that is how muscles are developed. In fact life is another name for learning. As long as we live, we need to learn and we have to learn. I think God gives us this life, to know His world, including ourselves.

> "I am grateful for all of my problems. After each one was overcome, I became stronger and more able to meet those that were still to come. I grew in all my difficulties."
> -- J.C. Penney, businessman

What shall we learn?

Most of the time, what we learn is not in our hands. On our journey of life we will see phases and places which we never wanted to, but still had to move ahead. This the way any journey takes place. Our choice lies in what we want to retain or discard. Every

> In a way, life is about discovering what is within our control and what is not. We need to find this boundary and go beyond.
> -Mohit Tomar

moment of life gives us a plethora of learnings but we need to see their applicability in our lives. We do have a choice of creating experiences of the events which we go through. Every event is not an experience. Only when we reflect through observation, contemplate through our reasoning and imbibe new concepts in our memory that it becomes an experience. Our life is beyond our control but still very much within our control. What we want to learn and retain is totally our choice. It should bring positive and productive and worthwhile change in our psychology and personality. If a learning experience is not understood and utilized in our day-to-day lives, it has no meaning. The central point to any learning is the basic principles on which events and things move. It is elucidating the inter-connectedness of entities and effects of one on the other. It is to orient ourselves with this universe. Life is all about knowing ourselves and our world better. Only then we can be more comfortable with ourselves or our world.

Being in Order.

The order of life is its disorder. In the end, we need to bring a meaningful understanding of all our experiences. Life by nature is disorderly and messy. All our learning comes through haphazard events which we go through. We need to exercise our choice and creativity, in organizing the experiences we have gone through and the knowledge gained. As per the second law of thermodynamics, the entropy of the universe always increases. In other words, the universe always moves from a state of order to disorder. If we leave a room unattended for some days, we will see the room in a state of total mess with spider webs and other insects among dust and dirt. If a garden is left untended for some days, it will be full of weeds and overgrowth. The same is with our minds; if we do not deliberately work on it, it will harbor unnecessary and unwanted thoughts. We need to put in well-defined efforts to bring things into order. Knowledge is all about organizing and filtering ideas, innovations, opinions, beliefs and principles. Our mind works best and gets traction, only when it is not cluttered with unnecessary information and insights. Then only can it provide us the necessary movement on our journey of life. Yesterday, I was cleaning and organizing my house, and I think the critical task in it was to remove unwanted or obsolete stuff out. We need to keep auditing our mind and ourselves as a whole, to keep ourselves, updated and upgraded. All the obsolete and outdated thinking, reasoning, outlook and skills needs to be replaced with new and relevant ones. We need to strive for order in the disorder of life.

Learn to Liberate.

The core objective of any education is to liberate us rather than limit us. If we observe the early years in a child, all his learnings prepare him for life…walking, running, thinking, and so on. But as we grow, as an adult, education provides us certain skills to earn our livelihood and often along with this, wrong patterns of

> I am indebted to my father for living, but to my teacher for living well
> - Alexander the Great

life. Learning should provide us a better and bigger picture of ourselves and the world around us, so that we can deal with ourselves in a more comfortable and creative manner. The education should expand our personality and build our character rather than limit us.

Learn to Learn.

Most of the time we do not know how to learn. It is not about learning a few facts and figures. It is the ability to deal with unique and new situations of life. No life is a carbon copy of another life. Every life is distinctive with its new and novel problems. The best lessons of life are learnt by oneself, when we decide or choose what we want to learn, and also the meaning we make of it. We may go through similar situations, but again the various determinants are different. Case studies and previous knowledge can be productive, but can also be counter-productive. Can a leader of an organization copy a previous template to deal with a new situation? Can a military commander use the same set of tactics in a new situation? Can one live his life by reading and initiating a biography of a famous personality? We may get certain cues and clues, but we need to apply our inner being, that is our own self-awareness, wisdom and intuition to deal with the process of learning.

> The only person who is educated is the one who has learned how to learn and change.
> -Carl Rogers

Time to unlearn.

When I was at school, I thought that good grades in different subjects is the key to living a good life. But when I faced real problems in day-to-day life or otherwise, I felt the need of different skills. These days such skills are called life skills. Whatever we call them, they are more important to life than any other kind of knowledge. Ability to lead troops in battle through chaos and crisis, does not come from traditional subject knowledge but the knowledge of life and living. Then only we can deal with lives. Ability to deal with the issues of a marriage and divorce do not come from any school or college. Ability to survive and stretch under the stress and strain of situation needs a strong character full of grit and determination, which is developed and nurtured only through solving real life problems. No knowledge is ultimate. Every knowledge itself is questionable and debatable. The people who think they know it all, are doomed. Even organizations fail when they stop learning. I have a deep interest in reading, but recently, I face a difficult situation, when the large collection of books ceased to answer my questions of life. They helped me to deal with

> 'The illiterate of the 21st century will not be those who cannot read and write, but those who cannot learn, unlearn, and relearn'.
> -Alvin Toffler

various difficult situations in life but also failed, at some points. It was time to look beyond and inward too, for getting a bigger picture God has set for me and the lesson he wants me to unlearn, learn and live.

Recalibrate the Mindset.

Learning can happen only when we are ready to learn. A pot kept upside down in rain will not get filled. One needs to be teachable and open-minded. Strong observation and reflection are the key to making a sense of what is happening around us. Whatever we go through, reading, watching, listening or activities, only when we take notice of it and reflect over it, we can draw out the learning involved. Only a positive mind will draw positive lessons. In our schools, we are repeatedly told that life is full of competition and only the fittest survive. I do agree that fittest survive but that does not mean that we need to pull others down. We must be the best of ourselves and we will thrive. We must introspect how we can contribute to this world, in terms of our research, dance, music, projects, ideas, literature and so on, as such we do not need to compete with anyone except ourselves. In fact, this will get us more collaboration than conflict, which is so unique to human life.

> I never learn anything talking. I only learn things when I ask questions.
> -Lou Holtz

At the end, I can say, that life is a journey full of learning and unlearning, a discovery of what works and what does not, and who is with us and who is not. It is all about making sense of the world around us to deal with it in a more meaningful and methodical manner.

"Self-education is, I firmly believe, the only kind of education there is."

— Isaac Asimov

8

Act to Lead

If your actions inspire others to dream more, learn more, do more and become more, you are a leader.

John Quincy Adams

Once again I would like to re-iterate and ponder again over two questions: 'Is life random or orderly?', & 'Is life real or unreal?' First, let us discuss the puzzle of order in the universe. If we observe and study the universe, we see that disorder or randomness are common throughout. However, this disorder coalesces to form an order. If we see the movement of a dust particle in the sunlight, which is called 'Brownian Movement', we can elucidate the randomness in the way it moves. This randomness extends throughout the universe, and is itself considered the order of the universe. Many scientists have struggled to define the laws which govern this randomness, or to find an order in it. The more the energy acquired by a material, through heat or movement, the greater the increase in randomness. Second, thanks to the discoveries of quantum physics, which proved that what we see or touch is nothing but emptiness, the structure of an atom is such that it is majorly empty till the fast haphazard movement of electrons makes it something real. Together such atoms combine to make matter.

If randomness or disorder turns into perfect order, I think the universe will cease to exist and collapse. Also if the movement of all electrons and other sub-atomic particles stops, the intra and inter-nuclear force, will come to zero and all the matter will fall apart and cease to exist.

So, we can conclude that randomness and nothingness is universal and is the 'reality' of universe. These two lessons of universe have direct implications in leadership studies and practice.

During my military service, I was trained to take decisions and act to prove my decisions right. I soon realized that decision-making and courageous action are central to any setting in the domain of leadership. Life is random and disorderly, but humans always have an inner craving and urge to find order in everything and draw patterns & conclusions, to help them to predict the future and take decisions in their best interests. We always struggle, study and secure certain laws, principles, theories and hypotheses to help us make decisions which do not lead us into problems. We do our best to study universal laws to guide us on a journey of least resistance and maximum results. Then, the power of action is most pervasive in the practice of leadership. Leaders believe in and demonstrate action. They are always in a state of movement and mobility. Our lives themselves are about movement. A person is known by his decisions and actions, that he has no worth as a physical body, if he is not taking decisions and actions. As long as humanity exists, dreams, aspirations, inspirations, sacrifices and all other tales of human endeavor will exist. Even our body is majorly empty, but the sub-atomic forces are very strong, as has been proven by invention of atomic bombs. Our body has so many inner forces and processes going on inside us all the time, how then a human being exist without this movement. Humanity is necessarily defined by this 'movement' of human beings. This realm of intangible forces and movements inside us in a way defines life and ultimately manifest in the form of our aspirations, attitude and actions.

Leader: Always accessible and visible

A military officer is always trained to take decisions, whether right or wrong, and take ownership and responsibility for same. Also, he needs to be visible to his troops all the time. He needs to be present everywhere all the time. Just like electrons which move at such great speed that they are everywhere and gives the illusion of solidness, a leader needs to exist in different dimensions at all times.

What is leadership?

More than a billion sites pops up when we google a definition of leadership. There have been a plethora of definitions elucidating the meaning and implications of leadership, but one definition which truly pins it down is from General Bernard Montgomery. "Leadership is the capacity and will to rally men and women to a common purpose and the character which inspires confidence."

How do we lead people? Leading is essentially an 'action'. Nothing inspires people more than action, which is why the term 'Lead by example' emerged. Our actions define us. People buy in to what we do, and not what we think or say.

The true test of a character is when we work on a plan with persistent and consistent efforts. Doggedness and determination are exhibited through action not through thinking or words. Deliberate thinking is crucial to decide our course of action but everything cannot be planned and prepared before moving on a journey. The best way to decide further action is to act. If we keep moving, we will get the road ahead. The insight of "Chaotic action is better than orderly inaction" – from the book 'In search of excellence',

> A leader is a dealer in hope.
> —Napoleon Bonaparte

has always inspired me to action. We cannot be a hundred per cent right before execution of our plan. Common people try to make fool-proof plans and never try. But leaders tap into their faith and intuition, and take the leap, and keep getting directions on their journey of action.

The power of action is so pervasive that even prisoners escaping a fortified penitentiary, or criminals giving shape to big crimes, have been able to get into books, movies and discussions, since they stimulate the same feelings of awe, amazement and admiration as the world's biggest leaders. A human being is naturally wired to get stimulated to action when he is exposed to instances where human beings have been stretched to their maximum, and their souls have taken over and exhibited the natural powers a human is born with viz. determination, daring and endurance.

A leader creates his aura through his action. He is obvious, open, overt and omnipresent for all his people. He is always available to them. He starts living his life on a higher plane where he transcends his personal life and the life of the ecosystem becomes his life. He starts thinking about the overall good rather than personal or petty goals.

What should a leader do?

Before going further, I want to make one thing clear, that leadership is not only the responsibility or privilege of a selected few, like ministers, CEOs, military officers or reformists. It is an essential

> Before you are a leader, success is all about growing yourself. When you become a leader, success is all about growing others.
> —Jack Welch

skill required by all in domains like self-effectiveness, relationships, families, societies and the workplace. All leadership thinking and skills to lead a prosperous and productive life. Leadership is all about creating a conducive environment for peace, performance, production and overall pleasantness. A leader is one who deliberates, demonstrates and does the needful for people to get stimulated to action and follow the team's vision. He creates conditions wherein every team member believe in the same values and follow the same vision.

- **Deliberate**

  Alone or with expert advice, the leader does a great amount of home work on the clarity on his concept. The vision is tested and thought over again and again with relevance to its requirement and reason. A leader is always clear on the concept on which he intends to work.

Mahatma Gandhi worked for five years to understand and update himself about the profile of the country, in terms of its people and their problems. During this period, he maintained a low profile and wandered as a common man to know the roots and reality of this country. This phase of his journey was to learn and conceive a plan. The gestation period was well taken care of before the idea was delivered to the real world. The idea of mass awareness and mass movement needed to be developed to full clarity before being launched.

- **Demonstrate**

  Once the idea is conceived it needs to be delivered or demonstrated to the real world and needs to be loved, liked and lived by the people. People need to buy into the idea voluntarily. We cannot force someone to love something. This is the real test of the leader in terms of his belief and faith in his concept and he truly needs to be spiritual to possess such a strength. No new idea was accepted instantaneously by the common man. Even the developments or introduction of new theories in different subjects were put down in the beginning. But the love for people and good intentions for the whole, wins over the people.

  Mahatma Gandhi, when he introduced the concept of freedom to the common people who were used to a life of humiliation and dishonor under British Rule, they were not ready to accept it. He had to create the awareness and make them ready to accommodate the new concept of freedom to their intellect.

- **Do**

  All creativity and concepts are justified when they are tested in real life. Ironically, we meet great thinkers with great thoughts every day but their ideas and insights goes to the grave with them without seeing the justice of its trial through action on it. The leader needs to act on his concept with courage and conviction. The ideas are bound to fail but at the same time, will open window to a new idea. That is how all developments in different engagements, in different eras have taken place. Remember, that everything is created out of nothingness, just due to movement or action of electrons. In the same way, a leader and his team takes massive action in face of all dangers and disasters. Action is critical to leading and even living. No action, no life.

When Mahatma Gandhi started the mass movements all over the country, he faced many challenges. He was defying the order (or disorder) of the day, to bring in a new order. That is a painful

> A leader is one who knows the way, goes the way, and shows the way.
> John C. Maxwell

process, as always a great deal of resistance was faced. But it was not only the British yoke that he wanted to remove from the hapless Indians, but wanted to bring a greater change and welfare to the society. He wanted to restore dignity and honor to the life of his countrymen. His concept of "fighting" using non-violence was unique and soon spread ubiquitously. Today he is remembered not only in India but many countries for his courage and character.

What is not leadership?

Being a Leadership Trainer, many a times I am asked about how many leaders we have produced. It is just like asking a military person as to how many people he killed during his service. It is the general perception of the common populace to think leadership in terms of authority, power and position. However, leadership

> The test of leadership is not to put greatness into humanity, but to elicit it, for the greatness is already there.
> -James Buchanan

is a journey on the path of self-awareness and self-development. It is about knowing oneself better and ensuring peace and prosperity for oneself. Only then can a person move ahead to add peace and prosperity to society. There cannot be parameters in terms of measurement or matrices to locate where one has reached on this journey. It is to be felt by the person, he has to be his own critic and coach. On this journey, he is not required to quantify and qualify. The power he gets is too massive and is beyond measurement. He looks just like a person in deep meditation seems to the outside world. He needs to know what he is doing and why he is doing it before the rest of the people knows. Awareness cannot be measured on any scale; so is leadership immeasurable.

The role and reasoning behind leadership has to be looked at in a different light. Just like the role of the army is not to kill people but to safeguard a

> The key to successful leadership today is influence, not authority.
> —Kenneth Blanchard

country against any kind of aggression or unrest and to ensure overall peace. In fact it is its responsibility to preserve and sustain life through its hospitals and 'weapons' in its own or alienated areas because that is 'right'. Today the dimensions of war have changed and the country that will win is the one who has provided more education to not only its own people but people around. No weapon is powerful enough to annihilate the section of population which has been denied justice and welfare.

In the same way leadership is not only about position and power. Real authority comes from love and affection for the people. Even the governments only which took care of

> A great leader's courage to fulfill his vision comes from passion, not position.
> —John Maxwell

their people survived, so how can a single leader without taking care of his people's welfare and well-being think of sustainable growth and development? Leadership is all about the larger good or greater cause which can bring growth and development for all and create an environment conducive to realize human potential to its fullest level.

"Civilized society exhibits five crucial traits; art, peace, beauty, truth and adventure; without which civilization is in full decay" by Alfred Whitehead

Leadership is permanent and pervasive

Power and position are relative and temporary, but leadership is not. A true leader is recognized and respected by all at all times. He does not need

> One measure of leadership is the caliber of people who choose to follow you.
> Dennis A Peer

any position and power. People follow him because they want to. His actions inspire them and they believe in his intentions. The intentions are the most overt thing although they may seem to be hidden. Even a toddler can sense our intentions. True leaders live a wholesome life and they go beyond personal and public life, work life balance and image management. They are loved by people for whatever they are because of their true and genuine intentions. They do not need personality development courses or need to possess great skills of oratory.

Leadership is about people.

The tasks and traits of leadership transcends boundaries of cultures and societies. They are the same across the globe and are deep rooted in the right intentions and initiatives. Leadership inspires and influences the entire human

> "You manage things; you lead people".
> Rear Admiral Grace Murray Hopper

race to further action. It is not only about doing good but also about making people good. It is all about people and their welfare in the long run. Even if it brings discomfort and discouragement in short run, it ensures long term benefits and blessings. It is about care and love. Leaders are hard task masters for themselves and their teams, thereby growing them and adding value to them. It is not about cheap popularity or being liked, it is about thinking and caring for the whole system, and working on what is right for long term sustainability and success. A leader maybe questioned and disliked initially but sooner or later his true and right intentions emerge and gain the popular support. Many such change agents have been identified, even after their deaths.

Leadership lays the future

Leadership is the future department of any organization or society or even a person. It is the agency which decides their

> "Leadership is the future department of an organization".

shape and size in the future. In every setback and failure, it sees the learning and lessons to move on. In every crisis, it sees the aesthetics to build on. It is an unrestful and turbulent place, a place of high energy and enthusiasm, from where the intangibles of vision and values radiates to his team and the world around. The leader is like the cosmic body from whom emanates the vibrancy and vitality for the complete organization. All the people feel charged in his presence, and get stimulated to massive action.

What does it take for one to become a leader?

I think everyone is a leader and the burden of leadership lies on each and every one. We all are born to be leaders and to live as an indispensable part

> The quality of a leader is reflected in the standards they set for themselves.
> Ray Kroc

of this ecosystem or the entire cosmos. We have our own individual roles and responsibilities to ourselves, and to the world around us, which we should fulfill responsibly. The burden of finding those roles lies on us, as to how we can contribute or where we can fit in the machinery of this world, to make it run smoothly. We need to find our true calling or our finest hour by ourselves. By birth, we are all geniuses with great powers, but we limit ourselves through the programming done to us by our environment, as to what we can or cannot do. It is only we ourselves who can find our true potential. Ironically, the most logical and reasonable people limit themselves most. Eccentric people who act and are identified by unique eccentricity shows the way to the logical people and sets standards of new logics. If we see a child playing, he displays all the natural traits which a leader should have viz. big dreams, strong determination, innocent persistence, deep belief, bouncing back from failure, people-oriented, unwavering high energy and thinking in terms of abundance. They truly possess the character which makes people feel happy and content when they look at them.

Leadership is an act of love

Leadership is truly an act of love and as such works to grow people and organizations. Love is always about the loved person and centered on acts to make the loved one more independent rather than dependent. A true act of love is to make people grow to their fullest potential. As such, the essence of leadership is to work on and for people to make them independent. At last the leader becomes dispensable. It is to mentor and coach people in such a manner that all the knowledge, skills and wisdom are passed down and the followers move on their own journey of self-learning and leadership. Leadership is about creating leaders. This aspect of leadership has also been covered in the chapter, 'Leave a Legacy'.

Going the right way and taking people along, to a worthwhile destination or at least on a worthwhile journey is all about leadership. It is living a life beyond self. Going on the journey of life in coherence with the complete ecosystem is essentially leadership. The most cherishing and fulfilling journey is the one through which we discover ourselves. However, on this journey the end goal of all our discoveries and decisions is to find our true self's relation to the world around us.

Leadership is solving problems. The day soldiers stop bringing you their problems is the day you have stopped leading them. They have either lost confidence that you can help or concluded you do not care. Either case is a failure of leadership.

— Colin Powell

9

Develop your 'Specialness'

"Don't compare yourself with anyone in this world...if you do so, you are insulting yourself."

— Bill Gates

As humans, we are quite similar to our evolutionary ancestors, due to the fact that we need and like to be a part of society for our survival, safety and social needs. But we have moved on and imbibed new dimensions into the purview of our life. As humans, our life is majorly dictated by our instincts for self-concept, self-esteem and self-actualization. We also need to stand out and show our "specialness". In fact, as humans we put our life in danger and take risks to prove our worth, to get recognized and be respected. On the journey of life, one of our goals or challenges is to find our true worth or our true identity. Somewhere deep in our hearts we all want to make a difference, and a deep impact, on this world. This is our natural instinct and cannot be overlooked.

On one hand, we like to be part of a winning team but on the other hand, we want to stand out. We find people with whom we relate to in any manner, who like to see the world in the manner we see it. We choose organizations to work with, a life partner to live with and friends to enjoy life with. But at the same time we search for our own identity, the 'real me', who is different and unique. At best we are discovering ourselves…….essentially our 'specialness'.

What makes us special?

By birth we are different but it takes a great deal of determination, deliberation and diligence to make us special. We become special, when we introspect and interrogate ourselves to find our true calling and work incessantly and seamlessly to develop ourselves to our fullest potential, in our chosen fields. We need to excel and

> "You are the only you God made… God made you and broke the mold."
> — Max Lucado, Cure for the Common Life: Living in Your Sweet Spot

deliver our best. Nothing less than the best. Above average performance does not earn us specialness. We need to be recognized by what we do. Our professionalism and proficiency lead us to set benchmarks against which all other related efforts and people are assessed.

When we think of the country, Jamaica what comes to our mind? Of course great athletes. When we think of the automotive engineering which country's name pops up in our mind? Germany. Similarly when we think of Yoga, we think of India. When we think of great education, Oxford and Harvard cannot be missed. When we think of supreme sacrifices and professional competence, we think of Navy SEALs or British SAS.

As is visible from such examples, specialness is a journey. It is a time consuming and endless journey on the path of excellence, in fact, nothing less than excellence. Specialness cannot be a goal but helps us to set goals. All the above examples have created the specialness through decades, if not centuries, to provide the best and extra of what is expected out of them. It is the extra efforts one has done on oneself, day in and day out, to live one's cause which inculcate or instill the desired specialness.

Why to be special?

An average life is not worth living. A person must do his best in every sphere or domain of his life. He should add more life to his everyday of living. Our biggest workplace or workshop is 'we' ourselves. We need to

> "There is nothing noble in being superior to your fellow man; true nobility is being superior to your former self."
> — Ernest Hemingway

discover and re-discover ourselves every day and every moment, then only we can work on ourselves. Excellence is a habit, and a person doing good in one domain, by default will do well in other spheres of his life. A high self-concept will propel one to do well in all dimensions of life. If we are not growing and developing to a new being every time, we are virtually dead; walking and moving around while waiting to be buried. An urge to be special brings the best out in us. It helps us to be a responsible employee, family member or a citizen. It propels us to put in effort and endeavor to learn, work and grow.

Even organizations and countries can go to great extent to preserve their sense of specialness. My military service very clearly exposed me to the specialness of the Indian Army, by virtue of which, soldiers make supreme sacrifices during call of duty. Today I can proudly say that I have been a part of such a great organization. In fact, most people join an organization or an association for its 'specialness'.

What one should do to be special?

Specialness is a spiritual dimension of a human being. Since we share a part of divine energy in us through our soul, we all have something special within us. As I mentioned earlier, we just need to question ourselves and discover it. There

> "Brightly burning passion is the releasing of your essence, your specialness and your gifts to the world."
> — Bryant McGill, Simple Reminders: Inspiration for Living Your Best Life

is something in us, which always wants to be recognized and known. This something needs to be discovered and developed.

- **Clarity of concept**
  Whether as an individual or an institution, we need to gain clarity with regards to our concept. Self-concept has to be very clear in terms of what we want to become, what we stand for, what we are doing, where we have to go and so on. We cannot excel at something which we do not understand.

- **Belief in the purpose**

  A deep belief and faith can only lead us to action on a grand scale even in face failures and setbacks. We need to discover and submit to the true calling of our existence and consider it is as a divine cause, a big purpose as if God wants us to do fulfil this purpose.

- **Massive Action**

  Great accomplishments are not achieved through average effort. We need to submit to our purpose or concept, and sacrifice ourselves beyond our limits. All research, inventions, discoveries, compilations and performances are achieved through cumulative efforts extended over a long period of time. There are no short cuts to excellence.

- **Re-innovation and Re-invention**

  For anyone to become special he has to become his own biggest critic. Self-assessment and self-directed improvement is crucial. It is better to be self-critical before others criticize. One needs to update himself before one becomes redundant. Only through continuous improvements, both marginal and radical, we can improve our selves or our products and services and deliver more than requirements or expectations of our stakeholders.

- **Make others feel special**

  If we are treating our stakeholders, whether customers, relations, colleagues, employer or society, as special; we become special. We need to take care of them, love them and empathize with them. If we understand them, we can serve them. The intention to serve with the best, is the surest way to be special.

When I started my corporate career in banking, the most frequent question I was asked by the customers was how the products and services of my bank are better than those of others in the market. In short, they were asking about my specialness. Every customer or client in any setting is looking for this specialness. In today's fast changing world we need to provide something different and extra, every time. We need to be more and matchless.

How to stay special?

Repetition is the Key. When an individual or an institution is recognized by what it does or deal in it, they are developing their specialness. They need to live the concept day-in and day-out. Every decision and action need to exhibit the concept repeatedly. When athletes from a particular country wins Olympics repeatedly, the country is identified with running.

- **Act to Demonstrate**. Words and intentions are not enough. Anything to be communicated needs to be visibly exemplified. When a beverages company withdraws its stock from the shelf due to a single faulty can of juice being noticed in the market, it speaks on its specialness in taking care of people's health.

- **Evolve to Endure.** To be irreplaceable and inimitable, one needs continuous self-improvement. Being relevant to the time can only ensure one his exclusivity and distinctness. Specialness is essentially excellence and not being 'different' or 'extra'. If a company is making cars, it need to provide more secured and safe cars through innovative engineering, which surpasses all the industry standards. It does not mean to provide something different or extra but only a better version, in terms of thicker chassis, more safety rods or more air bags. It is like a hotel providing one good and comfortable pillow rather than a large number of uncomfortable pillows.

Developing our specialness is a virtue

The burden of specialness can stretch one to his or her limits. It is the source of all inspirations and initiatives. We all want to be known for who we are. As such, we need to show what we can do and can offer to this world. How people see us depends on, how we see ourselves. Before others treat us as specials we need to recognize ourselves as specials and develop our specialty. We are not here on this planet by chance, lots of events took place for our soul to take human form here. Every human born on this earth is a result of millions of years of evolution. Even earth has evolved for billions of years to get ready to provide life to us. When we take the form of human we need to compete with millions of sperms and survive the thick and thins of so many uncertainties. A high degree of suitability and fitness is essential. A divine intervention is crucial. As such, I am proud to be a part of this human race and fully understand the responsibility of ourselves to grow and develop on journey of specialness and not just survive.

Before we want to be known by others we need to know ourselves, for what we should be known or remembered. We need to ask ourselves what is the first thing that comes to

> "Each of us is a unique strand in the intricate web of life and here to make a contribution."
> — Deepak Chopra

our mind when we think about ourselves. How do we identify and recognize ourselves? How can we be unmatched, unparalleled or unequaled? What is the unique being in us? I think any job interview or date invitation should deal with just one question: what is special about you or me?

This specialness is the key to a change or making a difference in any setting. A special person always has his presence felt

> "I don't get paid to be nice. I get paid to be right."
> — R.L. Griffin, Seamless

not only through kind words and keen thinking, but most importantly through action. He becomes indispensable and incomparable through his excellence. Only a special person can be a change agent. It reminds me of the Wright Brothers who brought change not only in the way we travel but how we think. It ushered in a new field of affairs for the human race. New dimension of war, explorations, sports, and other adventures developed. They were special people who are today identified with flying.

Specialness entails love for self and others

Only when we love ourselves and others around us we can develop our specialness. Emotions of hate, jealousy and envy cannot bring out this divine gift. We all exist in close communion with this universe and cannot stay healthy while in conflict with it through our negative emotions. It is our love for self and all the stake holders in our lives that we can develop and demonstrate our specialness. A great purpose itself is the manifestation of love for self and all around us.

When Mantri Developers sponsored my expedition to Mount Everest, it brought out their specialness of dreaming and demonstrating on a large scale. The organization has not only changed the way India lives but also inspires youth in terms of leadership and love. Their care and support for my expedition gave me the necessary impetus to endure and experiment with one of the most extreme endeavors on earth.

The journey of life itself is special and cannot be bought or borrowed. It is unique for everyone and as such we need to responsibly move on this journey by developing and demonstrating our own specialness.

"Some people are special because they're princes or princesses; or queens or kings! Some are special because they're presidents and senators; or because you can watch them on film! But what is the stuff that makes any person special? That makes any person more special than the world and everything in it? That would be love. Once you love someone? They're special, they're important. You make them important, it's your love that makes them more important than the whole world and everything in it! And guess what? That kind of important is real."

— C. Joy Bell C.

10

Break the Barrier

"Don't let reality, get in way of your dreams."

— Anthony Liccione

It is true that we are a prisoners of our own thoughts and nothing else. We cannot move on the journey of life beyond the limits decided by our own mind. Our worst prison is designed and developed by our own thinking. Our limits of action and achievement are decided by the limit of our thinking.

As humans we are endowed with a great blessing, the capability to think, and also to think about our thinking. Thinking can be a great tool if used judiciously to our advantage but can be very detrimental if it works against us or goes beyond our control. We are uniquely equipped to decide what we want to think or how we want to think. The onus of how we want to use this tool is fully under our control. We have transcended the entire animal kingdom due to the fact that we can aspire and inspire and also stimulate aspiration and inspiration in other fellow humans. Being human is our biggest achievement and we just need to truly live as humans, dealing in all human affairs on this journey of life, to be great.

Breaking mental barriers is a to achieve new standards of excellence and evolution

Any time human race has extended the frontiers of its evolution, it has been preceded by a liberated mind. When we start thinking in terms of

> "Sometimes your belief system is really your fears attached to rules."
> — Shannon L. Alder

possibilities and prospects, nothing can hold us back. Before something exists in reality, it has to exist very clearly in our minds. It may happen that we are not able to create something we have thought of, due to some reasons, but there is no instance of human achievement, even the smallest, where something has been created without thinking. Thinking makes or breaks us as a person.

We all have heard about Sir Roger Bannister who was the first person to run one mile in under four minutes. For the first time in recorded history, a human ran at this speed. It was a great human feat. But the most interesting fact, is that his record stayed for only forty six days. It ushered the human race to a new standard of performance in sports and raised the bar by breaking the barrier.

A successful journey of life is all about breaking our own barriers and also of the human race as a whole. It is true that

> "Experience is an asset but also a great liability."
> — Mohit Tomar

a real freedom a person or a population can achieve, is the thinking where there is no boundary to restrict a person. The true prisoners are not the ones who are in a penitentiary but those who are physically free but limited by their minds.

A person with a liberated mind cannot be detained or restricted by physical barriers. We are much more than our physical being.

To subdue a person in the real sense, one needs to subdue his mind. The true defeat is the one, which is inflicted on the mind. Real poverty is not the lack of finances or other physical resources, but limited thinking. We are products of our thinking. We grow and develop according to the most prominent thoughts we hold in our minds. Mahatma Gandhi understood this aspect of being human and worked to break the mental prisons of his countrymen. The entire British Empire was not able to detain a free mind like Bhagat Singh. Subhash Chandra Bose may not have been able to assemble an army bigger than the British army but he was able to rally freedom within the minds of his people. The concept of freedom was introduced successfully in the thinking of his people. The role of all education should first aim to liberate the human mind, which can think without fear. Only a liberated mind can liberate others. The real destruction or defeat to a country can be brought only by destroying all its educational institutions, libraries, research centers, museums, and so on.

I have a keen interest in real life survival stories and military special operations. Every story gives me an insight in to the undaunted and unlimited human spirit which lies within all of us. All of them have been created by people with a tough and resilient mind, a mind so strong that they have refuted and rescinded the logic and reasoning of science. They have stretched the human body and its physiology to new levels of endurance and existence. They made biologist and doctors revise their logic and lessons.

In every domain, whether inventions, discoveries, explorations, construction or entertainment, we see barriers being broken every day, every moment. This not only provides us our specialness as human beings but also is

> "The world is not ready for some people when they show up, but that shouldn't stop anyone."
> — Ashly Lorenzana

important to our survival. If we study the evolution of life, breaking the barriers of thinking and action, was crucial to adapt and survive. Millions of years back, a piece of life, took a leap and moved out of the ocean to the land and established out a new way of life for the living kingdom. Subsequently, some brave animal took the initiative and pain of trying to walk on two legs to look for food in the distance, and initiated a new approach to move around and live. Every small or big step taken to break the barrier brought us to our present shape and size. Today, we fly in planes, lives in skyscrapers,

> "The path of least resistance is the path of the loser."
> -- H.G. Wells, author

converse with fellow beings across the oceans and so on, just because we broke the existing barrier to the ways of living.

Once when I visited the India-Pakistan border, I noticed a barrier on the road, which led into the other country, with India and Pakistan written on either side of the pole. I wondered why to create such barriers were created to restrict human freedom. The concept of country and counties is fine for effective management but should not create barriers to human thinking and travelling. I envy the birds flying over such barriers freely. Why cannot people just move around and enjoy different cultures, terrain, weather, and so on. The European Union is a classic example of breaking the barriers in search of prosperity and peace. The countries which fought world wars and endured millions of casualties are today the most coveted and enviable countries, in terms of prosperity and peace.

Why break barriers?

This is the most instinctive trait of a human life. We all like to rise and shine. We tend to get dissatisfied and stagnate very soon with a particular way of thinking and living. Newness is the source of energy and enthusiasm for us. We like new and novel ways to work on and imbibe them in our lives. Evolution is essentially a change in thinking and behavioral pattern. Every time a barrier is broken in any field, it catapults us to a new level of living. We relish it and regenerate through this. If we do not follow this natural discipline of life, we degenerate and die, if not physically then surely spiritually.

In our work, relations and above all, ourselves, we need to bring in something new to all; do something which we have not done earlier; and be something which we have not been. Performance in the workplace itself is

> "Excellence is the Result of Caring more than others think is Wise, Risking more than others think is Safe, Dreaming more than others think is Practical, and Expecting more than others think is Possible."
> — Ronnie Oldham

bringing something new and more to the table. The roles and responsibilities in relationships also need to revised and revitalized. If we are not growing ourselves, the things associated with us will also cease to grow. Our body works round the clock to renew itself. Cells grow and die and regenerate. But the responsibility of our mental, emotional and spiritual renewal lies with us. We need to work on re-inventing and re-adjusting ourselves.

How to break barriers?

- **Think in abundance.**

  Great achievers think in abundance. For them there is no dearth of resources; if not in reality, then in their minds. 'Everything is possible' is their way of thinking. It is like if one person takes more frequent breaths it does not create scarcity of oxygen for others. They do not think that someone has to become poor for someone to become rich. They like to compete with the best and to become better, because they know that there is more to achieve and more to improve. For them the journey towards perfection is never complete. There is always further to go.

- **Break the Rules**.

  Breaking rules does not mean to be indisciplined. It is about thinking in a new pattern or a new template to accommodate the vast imagination and inventiveness of human mind. Rules are designed according to existing ways of living, but we need to break them and set new rules, when we explore new territories. When the concept of plasma television was introduced for better visuals and vividness, the old methods of manufacturing had to be discarded.

- **Re-start and Re-boot.**
  A fresh slate is the best tool for original thinking. We need to break free from all previous knowledge and concepts and think afresh. Sometimes a concept reaches its maximum limit of value. After that we need to move on to something new. New ideas and innovations needs to be initiated. A typical example is space travel. When the race for space travel started, the jet engines, no matter how efficient, were of no use. The Rockets were introduced and new way of travel was unleashed.

- **Unlearn and re-learn.**
  Every theory and hypothesis has a shelf life and needs to be revised. The journey of Quantum Physics is a typical example of this concept. Every theory existed for a certain duration before being phasing out, but was essential to the development of a new theory. The organizations and people have survived and succeeded only when they discarded their earlier ways of doing things and incorporated new ones.

- **Set new records.**
  Events like the Olympics games are very overt methods of living this principle of life. The setting of new records and surpassing old records

is demonstrated in very clear and vivid manner. However, life may not be so clear, but we move ahead by setting new records. The dates are recognized by our achievements. The history of our lives is the series of our accomplishments and moments when we break certain barriers. We need to set new records not always in overt manner but in subtle forms like aspiring, aiming, thinking and acting. The days spent in enjoyment and fun are soon forgotten. However, I do not undermine the time spent in enjoyment. Spending time with self, with family and friends and with nature are crucial to our well-being and wellness.

What tools we have to break the barriers?

Breaking barriers is spirituality. One needs to connect to the divine power and calling. Our physical and mental capacities may need to equip us to do this. We need to connect with divine intelligence to get new ideas and insights. We need to harness the mammoth and gigantic power of our subconscious mind. When we push beyond our conscious mind, or seat of logic & reasoning, we need to tap into our subconscious mind to connect the divine power for our answers. There are certain tools that come handy on this journey.

- **Meditate**
  It is being one with self and being conscious of the self. One needs to feel self to awaken oneself to its fullest power and potential. It helps us to focus

and concentrate. If we can concentrate enough, we gain unmatched energy to do anything. Great achievers owns or trains their mind to focus. A wavering pattern does not lead us to extreme levels of performance. To break barriers we need a disciplined mind. Only a disciplined mind can accommodate faith and belief.

- **Visualize**

Great battles are won twice, first in the minds of the General and then on the actual ground. Olympians visualize the complete game in their minds beforehand to win. It helps to channelize our energy in to the upcoming task and perform at our best. It involves thinking about an event or an action with utmost details and feeling it with all our senses, as if it is happening or existing in reality. Mind precedes matter.

- **Affirm**

Positive affirmations prepare and program our subconscious mind to what we want. Do not tell your subconscious mind what you do not want. Just convey your true intentions in real time and it will work even when you are resting to help you provide it to yourself. Our subconscious mind just needs instructions through affirmations and it will keep working on them without our conscious knowledge. It provides knowledge and resources from the places where our conscious mind cannot take us.

Core of human learning: Ability to challenge self and create

It is worth thinking and re-thinking about how we can inculcate the habit of challenging self and surpassing the previous standards of self, in every child of ours. I am

> "People simply feel better about themselves when they're good at something."
> — Stephen R. Covey

thankful to my schooling which made me a congenial and conforming citizen, but it would have been great if there had been a subject study on creativity and innovation. No knowledge is worthy if it is not relevant to time and space we live. Applicability is the biggest motivation to learn. Teaching should not happen in isolation, it is a holistic process. The interconnectedness and interdependence of all subjects to spheres of life is important, and must be taught. Every subject had an impact on other subjects; they all evolve and grow together with implications on each other. Education should lead us to make sense and find patterns in how the universe function. Research and development should be at the core of any education. Any amount of knowledge should lead us way ahead into the unknown territory. Children should be taught and trained to delve, demonstrate and develop right from initial years of schooling. The faculties of imagination and initiative of children should be well-harnessed and honed to their maximum potential, for the human race to break barriers of past standards of excellence.

The best career is our life and its cause

In our culture, there has been a fad to make careers in engineering but still we are not producing enough research and development in the field. The faculty to create and innovate is seldom developed. In fact, engineers are engineers in their careers, but not in their minds. Moral courage is essential, to listen to the feeble voice from our hearts rather than succumb to social and cultural influences. I find it a sad state when people have to show their degrees and certificates to prove their qualifications and education. In continuation with the last chapter, I will reiterate that a person who is in 'full throttle' to break barriers is known by his actions as to who he is and what he can do. His every action proves it. He becomes one with his work, his work or his passion becomes his identity. Without

> Paint a masterpiece daily. Always autograph your work with excellence.
> -Greg Hickman

such focused and concentrated energy one cannot expect to break the barrier to set new standards of performance.

That reminds me of an incident when I was commissioned in the Army and a neighbor of mine told me that these days people do not want to marry their daughters to Army officers. I wondered firstly, I joined the army because I wanted to and not because I wanted to get married, and secondly, it is a poor state of affairs when people marry their daughters to certain careers rather than human beings.

To get ourselves and our generations, to break the barriers, we need to create an opportune environment, where people can have freedom to try new and novel ways of doing things.

Also, the onus lies on the individual to 'break free' from existing norms or the 'inertia' of thinking, before unleashing himself on the path of great achievements. To break barriers we need to 'break ourselves away from the routine'. The path is not difficult in reality as it is in our mind.

In 1947, when Chuck Yeager flew to set the record for the first supersonic flight, his experience was quite unique. Contrary to popular belief

> Rules are made for people who aren't willing to make up their own.
> -Chuck Yeager

that the body will explode at great speed and other such assumptions, he conveyed that moving into supersonic speed was very smooth and he felt a kind a smooth flowing motion. At times, things are not so difficult, as 'popular' belief makes it.

Breaking the barrier is not a onetime affair on our journey of life. It is not a goal to be achieved but a way of life. When we break barriers each time in every sphere of our lives, we not only re-invent ourselves but recreate a whole new society. As such, it is not a destination but a journey. To live such a life, the journey of life itself becomes the goal, and goes beyond failures and successes.

"When you disrupt yourself, you are looking for growth, so if you want to muscle up a curve, you have to push and pull against objects and barriers that would constrain and constrict you. That is how you get stronger."
- Whitney Johnson, Disrupt Yourself: Putting the Power of Disruptive Innovation to Work

---

11

Leave a Legacy

"Everyone must leave something behind when he dies, my grandfather said. A child or a book or a painting or a house or a wall built or a pair of shoes made. Or a garden planted. Something your hand touched some way so your soul has somewhere to go when you die, and when people look at that tree or that flower you planted, you're there.

It doesn't matter what you do, he said, so long as you change something from the way it was before you touched it into something that's like you after you take your hands away. The difference between the man who just cuts lawns and a real gardener is in the touching, he said. The lawn-cutter might just as well not have been there at all; the gardener will be there a lifetime."

— Ray Bradbury, Fahrenheit 451

Every journey of life is unique and leaves behind a unique trail or footsteps. Our unique personal signature or stroke is the crux of our journey. What we leave behind is our true self. Almost all forms of life pass on certain skills and expertise to their progeny apart from life itself, but the human race has taken it to an altogether new level. We have surpassed the natural order of evolution and brought our own parallel order. Today the way the human race has changed the face of the earth and is making an impression even on far away planets, is remarkable, as if the divine power has given some control to humans as well. Every race and every human has contributed to the unique signature of humanity being left everywhere. As human we leave a unique impression and imprint added to this evolution of human life. Human life goes beyond the natural instinct of survival and reproduction. We need to make our unique impression on this world and our unique contribution to our environment.

What is legacy?

Just the way we reproduce to pass on life, we go through a great deal of toil and turmoil to leave a legacy behind us. We all have an instinct to persevere. Perseverance for human is beyond life, it is about our ideas and ideologies which we leave behind. Many great leaders worked hard throughout their lives to leave great legacies, so much so that they ignored the continuance of their genes or life by having children. They lived on forever through their unique and important contribution to this world in terms of their ideas, innovations, inventions or ingenuity. They brought such evolutions and revolutions that they changed the order of the world for betterment and benefits of all. They were those strong headed and good hearted people who lived for a great cause and died in its pursuit. They found great peace and pleasure in their journey since their journey itself was a great achievement.

> "Are we being good ancestors?"
> — Jonas Salk

Nelson Mandela is a name which is synonymous with courage and strength. He truly proved that great wars are won through peace. All hate has to be ended with love. His life has left a great legacy of true grit and determination for a noble cause. He had one great weapon with which he defeated all… the weapon of love. He subdued his enemies

> The greatest legacy one can pass on to one's children and grandchildren is not money or other material things accumulated in one's life, but rather a legacy of character and faith.
> - Billy Graham

with his love and compassion. He exemplified how patience requires character and forgiveness needs strength. Loving those people who kept him imprisoned for twenty seven years takes great self-mastery and a high self-concept. Great personalities like him do leave great legacies. After his release and rise to power, he looked ahead for a higher vision of universal peace and prosperity for his country. He forgot and overlooked his personal feelings of pain, for a brighter future for all. Through his personal example, he inculcated a feeling of love, respect and compassion among his people, and rolled out a path for sustainable peace and prosperity for his country.

The human race has turned out into a civilized and creative race through pattern legacies, passed down through centuries. It has given us capabilities to create cultures, institutions and organizations. It helps us to preserve the wisdom and knowledge of our ancestors. We know from where to take it forward. It gives us our identities and our backgrounds. It provides us the necessary guidance and guidelines to operate from. It is something which has to be taken forward.

How do we pass on legacies?

We do not necessarily need to hold positions or power, to create legacies. It is the aspirations and inspiration, we leave behind. Any human in any role has the capacity to leave legacies. We need to work from within. The intended legacies

"To know how a person will behave tomorrow, we need to know what he was yesterday" are not to be told but to be lived every moment, only then they can be instilled into the next generation. It is the concept, standards, ideas or thought, we live and leave behind us. Leaving a great legacy, demands sacrifice on our part. For others to accept and believe in our legacy, we need to sacrifice ourselves in its pursuit. The legacy has to be so big that our individual lives becomes small in front of it. Our individual journey cannot contain it, and it has to transcend our own lives to affect other lives in a positive way. We need to go beyond our immediate benefits or short term thinking. Legacy is spiritual. We cannot create legacies through our body, mind or heart. The soul has to take over to create legacies, as both of them are indestructible. We need to overlook immediate pain and pleasure, to search and sow something so big and magnificent that it inspires people.

We all lead our journeys exploring new frontiers, but how do we ensure that our journey is taken forward? True death is the death of our thinking; what we believe in, what we stand for and, where we want to go. When we die physically, we still live through our thinking. The dreams, direction, discipline, and demeanor we leave, keep us alive even after

> Carve your name on hearts, not tombstones. A legacy is etched into the minds of others and the stories they share about you."
> — Shannon L. Alder

our physical death. That is why legacy is a spiritual work. We need to think beyond today or tomorrow, we need to care for generations to come.

It is not the void we leave at the time our death, but the values we lived by, the value we added to this world. After the sad demise of my grandmother, I realized that true love never dies. I still find her close to me and always with me. Her physical self may not be visible to me, but her teachings and guidance have always been with me. She always taught love, patience and compassion to me and all my siblings. Not only myself, but the whole town remembers her for her goodness and nobleness. I truly feel that she is still among us through her legacy. Also, I feel the pleasure of taking this legacy forward to the next generation through my training programs or bringing up the young ones in the family.

How do we live and leave a legacy?

1. **Dream**

   A dream is crucial for anything to exist in reality. We need to know what we want to achieve as humans as the human race. For any legacy, the ultimate aim or accomplishment has to be first borne in mind before it becomes a reality. Exploring new frontiers of discoveries and inventions, developing pieces of art and literature, protecting the environment, reformations and revolutions in societies and cultures, and so on, are different fields for human evolution. Every change or transformation is preceded by the awareness and knowledge of 'where we are' and 'where we want to go'. If we do not know what to live for then what can we die for. It is our dreams or vision, through which we leave our legacies.

2. **Direction**

   A dream can be realized in many ways. But the true essence of our legacy is the path on which we usher ourselves and others. It is the path we take to our destination. For example, there are a number of ways to become rich or generate profit for the organization, but which path we take, ethical or unethical, is crucial. The ends and means are both important to a legacy. To give direction to others and generations to come, we need to be self-directed and self-controlled. To leave a great legacy for others, we need to live a life of virtue ourselves. A rudderless ship or boat cannot carry passengers to any destination, it will go in circles. We have to have clarity and courage of following a set direction against all odds and oppositions. We need to find our own direction before giving direction to others in any setup.

3. **Discipline**

The set of values, ethics and morals a person follows and uses as a frame of reference, is crucial to the domain of one's legacy. It is the unwritten discipline which has been passed down from one generation to the next which has brought us to this level of civilization. For a person to follow a good code of conduct, we do not necessarily need the police, laws and courts. We do not need external force or restrictions to be good. It is the inner enlightenment and innate discipline which regulates us to 'goodness'.

4. **Demeanor**

Our day-to-day behavior is the essence of our dream, direction and discipline. We need to exemplify what we believe in and stand for. We are what we do. Our daily routine defines us. Our legacy is conveyed through our daily routine. It is the most overt and obvious form of communication. Live, live, live and live what you want to leave behind or be known for. A legacy is preceded by years of repetition of a behavior, exemplifying the unbreakable belief in the concept or idea.

In fact, these were the reasons why a leaders like Mahatma Gandhi stimulated people "to be the change one wants to see in the world".

How legacy helps us?

Legacy brings sustainability. It brings permanence and perseverance to an idea. How far a generation will reach, depends on the legacy it is carrying. There have been institutions which have stood firm through all kind of chaos and crisis of wars, famine, floods and earthquakes. Religious and educational institutions are such examples. Organizations which have lived their vision and values through thick and thin of time, have sustained crises and endured.

In my uncle's family, five children became doctors, due to the legacy left by the eldest child. She rolled out a path for others to follow, by giving dreams and direction to her siblings. I myself live the legacy

> The final test of a leader is that he leaves behind him in other men, the conviction and the will to carry on.
> —Walter Lippman

of carrying my profession as a cause, as has been passed on to me through the books of my favorite authors. It gives me the standards to sustain. It is not an order passed down to people but a shared belief and emotion. The emotional connect has to be present to make any concept a legacy. As such, to leave a legacy, we need to be truthful, honest and steadfast to our ideals. We need to make sacrifices for them, love them, only then it can move others. We need to be repetitive but not driven by routine. We need to live our legacy every moment but it should be lined and laced with our passion and enthusiasm for it.

Recently, I met a person named Dinesh and was inspired by the way he came forward to remove a branch which had fallen on the road, due to heavy rains and a storm in Bangalore. Traffic was obstructed and led to a jam. A college student,

> A child is your legacy. What better thing can you do in life than put a really good person in the world who's going to make it a better place?
> Alexis Stewart

Dinesh came forward to pull the branch to one side and encouraged others to come to help. During my conversation with him, I was touched when he conveyed that it is all because of the right values given to him by his mother. It is true, that if we are bound by the right values, we do not need the penal judicial laws to discipline us.

The education system should keep the 'righteousness' and 'moral conduct' at the core of the education. Education is all about living peacefully with oneself and others on this beautiful planet. Peace is not for the weaker ones but for the strongest. Only those who are weak and incomplete, who lack an identity and background, fight to make their presence felt and as such, disturbs the overall peace. Basic goodness and character is crucial for sustainable peace. We cannot have laws to make a husband love his wife, children love their parents, care for one's country, take ownership at work, and so on. We need to have the right legacy to be passed down through generations.

How to deal with bad legacies?

At times we are passed down bad legacies which adversely affect us. However, as humans we have the power to question and revise the way we live. We need to keep questioning the practices and principles we live on.

Traditions and customs need to bring justice and well-being to all. Malpractices like 'sati' and 'jauhar' had to be re-visited and rescinded. The legacies of reformists like Raja Ram Roy ushered a new order for our culture and justice towards women.

> All good men and women must take responsibility to create legacies that will take the next generation to a level we could only imagine.
> - Jim Rohn

The turnaround from wrong and irrelevant legacies itself is a great legacy. To refer to the poor girl's story, whom I mentioned in a preceding chapter. Filing false cases against a husband had not only shown a lack of responsibility and integrity, but also a bad legacy from a father to a daughter. The display of bad character had been the legacy to the daughter who reached a stalemate and did not know what to do next. Wrong intentions can never bring right outcomes. The woman's father died within a year after his deeds (or misdeeds) and guidance (misguidance) but the daughter is living is his legacy by fighting her husband in the courts. The legacy of hate and animosity never brought any good to her.

What is the first step to create a legacy?

Legacy is something to be taken forward. For everyone's comfort and ease of understanding, the legacy needs to institutionalized and well framed. We need to ask the following question of ourselves.

- Why should we be remembered?
- What shall we be remembered for?
- How shall we be remembered?

Working on oneself must always precede working on others. We need to be truthful and transparent with self. We

> History is the essence of innumerable biographies.
> - Thomas Carlyle

need to ensure clear understanding of the questions above, through well-articulated communication in terms of our words or works.

How to preserve the legacy?

Our history speaks a great deal about our legacy. Our country's or the world's history is one subject which I feel every child or adult should read, at every phase of his life. It encompasses every facet of human life and the human race. The wars and peace, sacrifice and betrayal, courage and cheating, vision and vengeance, economics and science, explorations and business, and so on. All the accomplishments and misfortunes of humans are conveyed to us through the study of history. If we want to know where we have to go, we need to know where we have come from. If we want to know what to do in future, we need to know what we have done in past. The patterns in our past give us an insight into our future. Otherwise, we cannot find the right path to take and which to avoid.

A small meeting in a room in Philadelphia initiated the war of independence for what became the United States. One push to a common man from a train in Africa, led Indian Freedom movement to a new level. Many such instances and incidents, convey a few things in common. Any race or group of people suppressed for long will have an adverse effect on all. We need to work and pass down a legacy for overall

> "If you would not be forgotten as soon as you are dead, either write something worth reading or do something worth writing."
> ~ Benjamin Franklin

peace and prosperity. Widespread peace is the first step to prosperity. Any section of society cannot be prosperous for long at the cost of others.

I hold great importance for museums and memorials, the way they help us to preserve and commune with our history. They are like the mirrors of our past. They play a remarkable role in connecting us to our past glory, achievements, failures and standards. They inspire us to further evolve on our journey of life as a human race. The roads and squares named after martyrs and great leaders, inspires us to act further and preserve their legacy.

Legacy is an indispensable aspect of our journey of life.

On this journey, if we have not moved enough people, then it is not worth travelling. Although, before moving others, before exciting others, we need to move ourselves. Our own excitement will excite other people. The traditions and customs which give the human race, our culture, organization or family its sustainable structure and size must be carried forward. A few examples of legacies in some organizations are worth taking note of.

- **Courage and sacrifice in Army**
  No organization preserves and protects their legacies like the army. My experience with the army taught me how far one can go to live and protect a legacy. Any officer joining the regiment is required to study and learn the regimental history with reference to its inception, accomplishments, battles, sacrifices, war heroes and people who served at various appointments. The soldiers and officers go to any extent to live this legacy, even if it requires them to make the supreme sacrifice of their life. Nothing should tarnish the reputation of the regiment which has been built and protected through the blood of so many valiant soldiers. Various institutions of the regiment preserve and pass on this history and

legacy to new generations of soldiers. People come and go, but the legacy remains. The Army through its regiments is always ready to serve the country in any manner, without any conditions or complaints.

- **Entrepreneurship and good values at Amway**
  In the corporate world, every company sustain itself through various good and bad phases, through their magnificent vision and moral values. Those who lacked it did not survive the ordeals of economic upheavals. The growth of 'Amway', not only in business terms, but the love and affection from people, is an example, how businesses can make a big social impact on people. It has added great value to society not only in terms of good products but by inculcating an entrepreneurial spirit in customers and giving them an opportunity to earn while spending. It changed the dimensions of business. Today people just love the legacy of the company and are willing to carry it forward by helping enough people to help themselves through financial incentives.

Even in our homes, we preserve awards, certificates, gifts, photo albums and other mementoes for the future, revisit and reaffirm our past achievements and future actions. They inspire us to act for the future and gives a sense of satisfaction for the past. They truly preserve our journey of love, sacrifices, hard work, vision and other associations.

Leadership and Legacy

Legacy is an indispensable part of leadership. The final step in any leadership endeavor is to make oneself dispensable. Leadership is making people self-dependent and self-learners to ensure sustainability. When a leader leaves, he does not leave a void behind but a great value-addition to his family, society or organization, which keeps them thriving for years to come. A leader's primary role is to empower and enrich his people through inspiration and initiative. The positive changes he brings to the processes and people are to live for a long time. Leaders do not create dependency but independence. They make people self-reliant. A leader takes the people or organization to a stage where he can comfortably move on, leaving them in sustainable health and happiness.

> The only thing you take with you when you're gone is what you leave behind. ~ John Allston

As humans we need to leave our legacy in every setting or role. We are not animals driven only by basic instincts, but are beings of higher order with higher order needs. Leaving a legacy is one such need. We all need to live even after our deaths through the ideas and ideologies we give and live in our lifetime. Our personal impression and mark is an important part of our journey of life. There has to be something unique about our journey worth remembering. If we live a worthy life, we NEED to leave a legacy behind.

True leaders don't invest in buildings. Jesus never built a building. They invest in people. Why? Because success without a successor is failure. So your legacy should not be in buildings, programs, or projects; your legacy must be in people.

Myles Munroe

12

Manage your 'Self'

"We should every night call ourselves to an account; what infirmity have I mastered today? What passions opposed? What temptation resisted? What virtue acquired? Our vices will abort of themselves if they be brought every day to the shrift."

— Seneca

The reason to live life always lies in the future. No future, no life. Whatever we do has its roots in the past but is meant to bear fruits in the future. We use our style of thinking and ways of toiling developed in the past. But every decision and action is routed to some particular purpose in future. And, whatever has to be done, must be done in the present. We cannot escape the present. We have to operate in the present frame of time and space.

What is more important, leadership or management?

The question has been dealt through various insights and intellects in different eras of time. In fact, this question can only be answered by posing new questions. What is more important, leadership or management? What is our understanding of these terms? And so on. However, the history in various domains has proven that we cannot lead what we cannot manage and also cannot manage what we cannot lead. If leadership is spiritual, management is the day-to-day affair. If leadership is about the future, management is about the present. If leadership is about finding and showing the way, management is about following the way effectively. If leadership is about 'why', management is about 'what' and 'how'. The journey of life necessarily demands both. One is incomplete without the other.

We need to manage ourselves to channelize our energies. To be effective, we need to be efficient too. If one know one's goal, he may achieve it someday by trials and error but that many take such a long time that the goal may lose its relevance to its purpose. If one has to go from Bangalore to Chennai, one may keep travelling in any direction and may hit Chennai someday. But this way of working may take him years to complete a five hour journey. On our journey of life we need to be efficient to be effective.

Right decision and diligence at the right time makes all the difference. If we know the purpose of our lives or the contribution we can make; we also need to know its relevance to the environment and time. If on our journey, we are not responding to the requirements of the day, we will not be able to carry on the journey for long. If it is rainy, we need to

> If you look to lead, invest at least 40% of your time managing yourself - your ethics, character, principles, purpose, motivation, and conduct. Invest at least 30% managing those with authority over you, and 15% managing your peers.
> - Dee Hock

wear raincoats; if it is sunny, we need to hold an umbrella; and if it is cold, we need to wear warm clothing. Similarly, if as a business organization, I am serving my customers with products which were obsolete a long time back, I will not be able to live out our purpose of existence. If as an education institution, we are not updating our curriculum so as to equip children and adults to the changing times, it will not add any value to the world and we will not be able to live up to our purpose. We need to orient and re-orient with the changing times and requirements.

Effectively managing self prepares us for the next big leap. In the military, we sort ourselves out or organize ourselves, after every battle or 'contact', to get ready for the next. It helps us to be in our control and in charge. Damage assessment in terms of breakage and injuries; checking and re-distribution of ammunition; orienting to the ground; discussing and deciding the next move; feedback to base, and so on.

Management brings sustainability to a person, institution or an organization. Even nations fall, when they are effectively led but not managed well. The well-constituted systems and structures provides a smooth flow. If all the parts and procedures of a machinery do not work in tandem, it will not even get booted. The synchrony and smoothness of all parts of the machinery ensures minimum heat loss due to friction. As such, servicing at right time is crucial. The world's most prosperous nations have fallen after the death of their leaders, when they did not possess a system based government which could provide a permanent and perseverant governance. A leader's role is not to make his people depend on him, instead it is to develop methods to make him dispensable even though his legacy may be continued. Being good is not enough, institutionalizing this goodness ensures longevity of an organization. Effective management ensures leadership effectiveness.

What is managing self?

It is the ability to harness and hone one's faculties in a manner so as to gain maximum energy and enthusiasm. If leading the self is the act of unlocking, liberating or awakening oneself; managing self is the act of directing, organizing and controlling one self. Managing self is to channelize our energy so as to gain maximum output from us. It is about the optimal utilization of self in service to our purpose of living.

Alexander the Great, is a name which has lived on as a source of inspiration and awe through centuries and countries. His remarkable leadership made him move lacs of people and conquer ninety percent of the known world of that time. However, his leadership trickled down from him and to all his people through his excellent self-management and systems of management, respectively. He managed well in terms of his goals and plans, tactics and tasks, structures and systems. He provided great clarity to his people in terms of who, what, when, where and how. Along with inspiration and ingenuity, he provided great logic and lucidity to his people.

Leadership gives us direction but it is management which gives us milestones. Leadership gives us development but management deals with our day-to-day doings.

Leadership cannot make an impact if it does not have a system of management to institutionalize it.

> Management is all about managing in the short term, while developing the plans for the long term.
> -Jack Welch

How to manage self?

Managing self is all about charging and re-charging self. It is to enhance our efficiency by dealing with self so as to get maximum output. The followings are ways to manage self in any capacity, as an individual or an institution.

- **Orient**

  The key to manage self is to first orient ourselves with our immediate environment, be it work, family, society or the whole world. Anything in our environment makes sense to us when we orient ourselves to it. In fact, any life born on the earth spends initial period of time to understand and adapt itself to its environment. We need to get comfortable with our environment and acquire a deep understanding of it. Just as we cannot fight what we cannot understand, we cannot live with what we cannot understand. We need to know self and the space we live in. How to do this? Explore, explore and explore. We just need to try, touch and feel.

  Whenever we face a difficult situation in life, we need to get oriented to the new and changed situation. If we are clouded or bogged down, we are sure to feel defeat. Our mental and emotional toughness is tested in only difficult times. How we behave in bad times, is our true character and true worth. The key to our mental toughness and tenacity is the ability to keep one's orientation. Among the story of extreme survivors whether shipwreck, abduction, captivity, or escape and evasion in enemy territory, the ability of not losing one's orientation is common to all survivors. In extreme situations, our mental and emotional resilience takes over our physical capabilities. Situations can break us physically, but when we break as a person depends on our mind.

> Nothing can stop the man with the right mental attitude from achieving his goal; nothing on earth can help the man with the wrong mental attitude.
> -Thomas Jefferson

In April 2015, on my way to Mount Everest, I was stuck in Everest Base Camp due to the massive earthquake which shook the country of Nepal. In the aftermath of this earthquake, a series of avalanches devastated the base camp, causing many casualties and injuries. Extreme fear and fantasies were generally prevalent but there were different responses from different people with no correlation to their physical size or shape. The ability to manage self in the extreme situations is a mark of our strength and personal leadership.

Mindset makes us or breaks us. It is how we orient our self and ourselves with day to day affairs which determine our overall efficiency. Our mind needs to be managed and fully under our control and direction. In other words, we call it our 'attitude'. It cannot be taught or bought but has to be developed through right association and actions. A positive attitude produces positive and profitable results. The only way to develop such an attitude is to 'fake' it till the time you 'make' it. The power of the subconscious mind gives us the tools of positive auto-suggestion to acquire such an attitude. Positive orientation is crucial in managing self.

- **Control.**

  The world has gone through wars, battles, skirmishes and terrorism just for the hunger of control by a few. It is sad to see that we fight outside to compensate for the lack of control we have within. We want to control things which are outside our purview and lead us to

  > "Anything that does not belong where it is, the way it is, is an "open loop" pulling on your attention."
  > David Allen, Author of "Getting Things Done"

  imbalances and commotion. And, in this pursuit we forget the pleasure of control over self. Control over self has nothing to do with abstinence or asceticism. It is not about giving away ones wishes and dreams. It is about taking charge of self. To be in full command of self, physically, mentally and emotionally. Those who are in control of self can never disturb the balance of nature and always bring long-term prosperity and peace.

  People are not able to control even their habits of unhealthy diet, alcoholic drinks and other wrong-doings, and yearn to lead and command others. How is that possible? Everything starts from within. A leader is the center of all action, what he does emanates outward like ripples in water. This center has to be perfect and positive. Anything negative in it will also get replicated exponentially among people. We need to control our finances and get free from bad debts. Debt is the new age synonym for slavery. Only a debt-free person can unleash his potential and passion. Health is another big issue which is addressed in the next chapter. Only a healthy person can enjoy the gift of life and its journey.

Control over one's emotions is the biggest victory a person can have over self. I do not mean to put a curb on the emotions but to understand and utilize them to our advantage. It is easy to be out of control but this can lead us to big problems. Remember, anger can be an expensive luxury. If we can manage our emotions we can save relationships, marriages, friendship, business deals, accidents and above all, our own health.

- **Organize**
  Whenever I clean and organize my house, I feel great liveliness and vitality within me and outside. The house becomes so comfortable with everything in place, all extra or unwanted things disposed of, and all the dirt and dust removed. I always lay importance on a lean and mean body, whether it is for a person and an organization. We should not

carry the burden of extra weight or size which eats into our efforts and slows us down. We must trim ourselves to bare essentials for higher efficiency. All unwanted things, whether extra weight on our body, unused items in our home or unutilized departments in our organizations, should be removed to be in the 'right' shape and size.

My military training groomed me to be organized in my daily life, to be in better charge of self. If we are organized, we do not need to bother or get bogged down in our day to day requirements.

> You can't grow long-term if you can't eat short-term. Anybody can manage short. Anybody can manage long. Balancing those two things is what management is.
> Jack Welch

We know what to get from where and how. The repetition of effort and depletion of energy is avoided. Even the teaching of how to fold a handkerchief and where to put it, serves me till date. No doubt such a vast organization has kept firm through peace and wars through centuries due to its strong organizational skills, where everything is accounted and audited. Every entity has a task to do and no entity is without a task.

Along with our actions we need to organize our thoughts. On an average we conceive fifty to seventy thousand thoughts per day, but they do not have any impact because of their randomness and as such they solve no purpose. However we can program and prime our brain to think about what we want to think and generate thoughts and ideas to solve our problems. We need to record these thoughts to reach necessary conclusions. Otherwise many great thoughts and ideas are lost as they are not secured or bonded on the paper.

- **Recharge**

  Any endeavor and effort, consumption of energy is a primary concern. We may feel tired and exhausted, and to carry on with our journey of life, we need to revive and restore the drained energy. How do recharge?

  ○ Revisit your inspiration
    Nothing energizes us like our inspiration. Revisit your inspiration through reading, watching a movie, meeting people, and so on. Spend time thinking, observing, studying and talking about your sources of inspiration. An inspired person is more energetic than a well-fed person. Food does not give us energy as much as our inspiration gives us.

  ○ Solitude
    Daily personal time helps us to know more about ourselves especially in relation and relevance to the present. It helps us to clarify and comprehend, the various daily issues and innuendoes. We have so many gadgets and software applications to be in touch with

people at great distances, but to get in touch with self we just need some personal peaceful time. We need to talk to ourselves and discuss various issues with self. This is the way to recharge for great decisions and actions in the moments ahead. Great leaders like Mahatma Gandhi, Nelson Mandela, Bhagat Singh and many more have created situations where they spent a great deal of time with themselves, on their way to becoming great leaders.

o Find your finest 'hour'
   One who knows his finest hour, can produce great results. It is the time when our body and mind is awakened to its maximum. It is the time when we feel most energetic and enthusiastic. Ideas and ingenuity just flow to us. At this hour we do not need to work hard, we just get into a state of 'flow'. We feel a kind of trance and great results follow. For some it is the early morning hours, for some it is the late night. I personally like to work at night when everyone is sleeping. In my case, I also find the time when I am driving very valuable, when I get lots of ideas and thoughts.

Managing self is essentially managing one's energy.

We have immense power to produce great results if we can channelize and concentrate our energies. We need to keep ourselves in the right shape and condition to be energetic and operate at maximum efficiency. We require high self-control and self-concept.

Yoga is a practice which brings communion between different aspects of our personality viz. physical, mental, emotional and spiritual. This collaboration and continuity between them unleashes a huge energy within

> "Your ability to generate power is directly proportional to your ability to relax."
> David Allen, Author of "Getting Things Done"

us. As the output of a machine is determined by the power created in its engine, in the same way the output of a person is determined by the power created from within. It is not the size, stature or status of the person which matters but the quality of personality he carry. A tall and big body may not be as energetic and enthusiastic as a middle sized body. Even a handicapped person who can unleash this energy is far more productive in life and pleasant to people around.

The daily practice of meditation leads us to harness the power of our subconscious mind to our advantage. If we can tap into the unlimited power of our subconscious mind, we can achieve the highest form of imagination, ideation, invention, ingenuity, and immunity in our body.

Time-management is a misnomer

A great deal of thinking and writing has been done on managing time but all of them lead to only one conclusion... we cannot manage time, as it cannot be bought, borrowed or begged. Time management is

> Effective leadership is putting first things first. Effective management is discipline, carrying it out.
> - Stephen Covey

essentially a goal setting process. We need to be clear about what we want in our lives, where we have to go. Our direction and destination decide our priorities. To pick up something we need to drop something. We cannot do everything, we just need to know or find out what we want in our lives and decide our actions accordingly. If all unnecessary actions can be obviated and we will be surprised by the amount of time we have. All great lives had the same limited amount of time available to them, but they knew where to spend it.

Delete the unnecessary, delay what is not urgent, delegate what can be done by others and do what is important. We cannot do everything and need to choose what is important, to be done

All our actions and decisions should lead us to our goals. A piece of time well invested will give multiple rewards and we will not have any dearth of time.

Life's journey is fast and fruitful when we are managing ourselves well, when we can manage our energy. Then only we can travel longer. Self-management is the key to a meaningful journey.

"As a rule, we must not be the slaves of passion; rather, we must be the possessors of great passions. Through passion commences power, but passions should not direct our paths; rather, passions should be our bridled horses, with us commanding whence and to they be directed. Our passions must not take their own courses; but they must be directed by us into which course they ought to take. Modern day people blindly follow the notion that to be slaves to their passions is to be free! But for one to be the Master of one's passions is to be not only free— but powerful."

— C. JoyBell C.

13

Harmonize for Health

Health is a large word. It embraces not the body only, but the mind and spirit as well;…and not today's pain or pleasure alone, but the whole being and outlook of a man.

~ James H. West

Health is the most abused and misused word in today's fast paced life. We do great injustice to our health while meeting the deadlines and demands of day-to-day life. Due to overuse and exploitation, our body snaps. It is not our big dreams or stretched goals which spoil our health but our mismanagement. When we are not able to manage ourselves, our health falls apart. Not work, but wrong-doings tire us. Not stretching oneself, but stressing oneself, exhausts us and ruins our health.

Any life at birth is healthy. We all are born healthy, but generally, we work (or do not work) our best to lose our health. In fact, health is not supposed to be attained but just maintained. We just need to live the natural order of life to maintain what we are born with. Our body is our interaction with this world or essentially our human experience. We cannot imagine enjoying this journey and live a meaningful life without having a great health. If we are in harmony with our path and place, we will be healthy. In other words, if on our journey, we plan, prepare and perform in relevance to the environment and situation, we will be able to endure.

Health is a vital dimension of life and leadership, it denotes our self-awareness and 'surround'-awareness. It shows our capability to stay in sync with ourselves and our surroundings. It is our ability to adjust and adapt to changing situations. A healthy individual grows stronger and stable, under changes and challenges, as per the natural order of life. Health is our ability to live to our true nature.

What is health?

It is the state of overall well-being and well-ness. Health is harmony. It is our ability to interact with our environment, outside us and inside us, smoothly, seamlessly and synchronously. It is how well we fit into this world or the overall eco-system. That is the fitness a person possesses. A healthy individual is one who can deal with the day-to-day affairs with ease and effectiveness. He can adapt well and adjust comfortably, to changing times. Health is not about looks but about life. It is about how well we live and last. It is the effective and efficient engagement with the eco-system of our environment which includes the weather, terrain, people, tactics and tasks we have to deal with.

Health is not only about our physical well-being but also about how we feel at heart and think with our minds. Along with a strong physical body, health encompasses a sharp

> To keep the body in good health is a duty, otherwise we shall not be able to keep our mind strong and clear. - Buddha

mind and a stable heart. It is a wholesome experience of life where body, heart, mind and soul, develop and are redeemed to the maximum.

A healthy person is always happy. He is pleasing to people around him and at peace with self. People get attracted to him, like iron fillings get attracted to a magnet. He possess as great security, stability and strength within and 'without'. Everything is in perfect balance, order or discipline. This balance gives stability, the essence of life. Inside our body, every day so many cells grow, compete and dies. The old and outworn cells are automatically replaced with new and vital cells. The discipline ensures that healthy cells stay and weak one wither away. This orderly competition is remarkable and required. At the same time, so many cells, organs and systems work in perfect collaboration to maintain the life. Whether it is competition or collaboration, both takes place in such a way that no garbage or residue is left behind, just to achieve the end-result of great health and sustenance of life.

Even a healthy organization or institution possesses the same attributes. They exist and evolve in perfect harmony within and with the environment around.

> Natural forces within us are the true healers of disease.
> -Hippocrates

People like to work with them and customers like their products and services. They showcase a perfect collaboration and competition within and also outside, and are in sync with the outside market. The big organizations need to learn so much from our body and its functions.

What spoils our health?

Our deliberate efforts, of not following the natural order of life and its journey, spoils our health. We work hard to destroy our health. Health is

> Sickness is the vengeance of nature for the violation of her laws.
> -Charles Simmons

a natural phenomenon just like rain and snow. We just need to ensure the right environment and setting for it to exist and evolve. We just need to maintain the natural order of life or living, to ensure a good health. It is not only about the physical body, we need to cleanse our heart and mind, every day and every time. Our wrong assumptions and interpretations about us leads to wrong decisions and actions which leads to wrong reality or results. It is ironic when people ask me, what I shall eat to reduce weight. This is not the natural order of life. This is contrary to even the common sense. We become overweight through the habit of unhealthy and undisciplined eating, and the only way to reduce weight is to work-out. Similarly, to reduce the pain and stress for the heart, one needs to apply tolerance, patience and forgiveness. To develop a strong and tough mind, one needs to solve problems and deal with difficult situations in life.

When we obstruct the smooth flow of the eco-system, everything else is disturbed. Today we pollute our environment with different kinds of waste, our body with unhealthy diet, our heart with negative feelings and our mind with wrong assumptions and interpretations. Only in a clean and clear environment, a healthy being can exist.

My military training, helped me to understand and imbibe discipline in various facets of my life. The training worked at the core of my personality and ensured the right character building. It made me to be mentally tough and emotionally stable. The physical training is just the route and not an end to ensure this. Only physical fitness is not enough to deal with the extreme environment in which military service happens. Not only I learn the power of mind and heart but also the fact that the soul is the essential 'me' and all other facets of ours are mere extensions of our soul. If our soul finds a purpose in our physical existence and endeavors, it will preserve us as humans on this earth and beyond. We need to live from our soul and listen to its call, even if it demands ultimate sacrifice. When we love what we do and find a meaning in it, then day-to-day stress does not tire us but strengthens us. We get tired through lack of purpose and not through a life of purpose.

The illusion of sickness

The various lifestyle health problems such as diabetes, heart attacks, blood pressure, cholesterol, and so on, are all results of our lack of leadership in living responsibly with our environment. We create them through our indiscipline. They can be avoided by understanding the true nature of self and our environment. As humans we are not supposed to eat food preserved with chemicals, or vegetables out of season, the result is the imbalance in the natural order and resulting diseases cause a natural fallout.

Even communicable diseases can be resisted by living in close communion with self. The body itself has a great natural mechanism of fighting infections through the bodies' innate immunity. But when we weaken this immunity through improper diet and lack of exercise, the infections are the natural aftermath of our indiscipline. A great deal of sickness can be avoided if we understand that body needs exercise and physical work just as we need to eat and rest.

What shall we do to have a great health?

We have to have a holistic approach to health. We need to deal with our 'whole existence' as one package. Body, mind, heart and spirit forms the complete package of human life and one cannot grow or develop at the expense of the other or in isolation. Life is incomplete without leadership. And leadership encompasses our overall effective existence and not the efficiency of body or mind. It is about living in perfect equation with rest of the world, and in the process adding value to both. Only effective leadership, our ability to behave responsibly to ourselves and our surroundings can ensure good health.

Ironically, we speak only about our physical body when we delve into the discussion on health. But body is a superficial aspect of ours. A human being is endowed with great tools of mind and heart. During our evolution the human race,

> The greatest miracle on Earth is the human body. It is stronger and wiser than you may realize, and improving its ability to self-heal is within your control.
> - Dr Fabrizio Mancini

we have lost or lessened certain physical capacities but compensated with great development of our brain and heart.

In almost all physical capabilities we are surpassed by other animals by large margin, but human beings still have the capacity to control all other lives through their sharp and strong mental acumen. As such, we need to take great care of this powerful tool we are endowed with.

If our hearts and minds are in order, our bodies will be in order too. We are defined by our thinking and our feelings. We evolve through the changes and updating of our thinking and feelings. How our body functions, is not only dependent on our fitness regime encompassing diet, exercise and rest, but most importantly, our mindset and emotional well-being. In fact, one's body is a slave to one's mind and heart.

- **Mind**

  The power of mind over matter has been proven again and again. I will reiterate, that our body is a result of our thinking. If we think healthy, we will be healthy.

  The power of the subconscious mind is massive and works without our active involvement. It is our link with divine energy. It works day and night for us without our knowledge. All our body's vital functions are run without our knowledge, at every moment. This mammoth tool is without any logic or cognitive power, like our conscious mind. We interact with it through our conscious mind. Whatever we believe in and affirm every moment, the subconscious mind takes it as a command

and works in its pursuit even when we are not consciously aware.

We all have experienced times when we are not able to generate ideas or solutions. If we give ourselves a little relaxed time, we automatically get ideas and solutions, without our active thinking. In the same way that works for our physical selves. For our physical body too, the doctors just operate and dress our wounds, but it is our mind which heals.

I myself have felt the power of mind in various extreme situations, such as military operations and mountaineering expeditions. Only a strong and stable mind can ensure a sound body. As such, we need to train and discipline our minds first before working on our bodies. I have some interest in long distance running, and the logic of long distance running is quite simple. The body will surely give up after some time and then the mind has to take over.

A cluttered mind cannot give clarity and calmness to a person. The confusion and chaos in the mind is an inevitable accompaniment to growth but it needs to be managed. We shall we do?

○ Reason
   We need to use logic and reasoning of day-to-day life to decide how we shall decide and do in different situations. Developing and disciplining one's thinking is crucial to take charge of our bodies and our world. We need

to understand the logics of how things work and use them to our advantage.

○ Rest
The mind in a relaxed sleepy mode, when it is free from all distractions and transactions, is the playground for great ideas and inventions. We connect to our subconscious mind in such a state. Mediation and prayer, all lead us to this state.

• **Heart**

Whatever the mind thinks and decides, the heart has to feel, for its effectiveness. The feelings behind all our thinking makes the difference. We need to be true and transparent. Whatever we think, we need to be true to ourselves.

The subconscious mind cannot accept a lie. The mind and heart need to work together to convince and command the subconscious mind. The excitement and enthusiasm about what we think and do is the key to the subconscious mind. Excitement and enthusiasm comes from positivity, passion and love. They have immense power and can control our environment. Even the inception of life happens when two partners get excited. Excitement is essential to the sustenance of life, too.

A heavy heart cannot ensure health of our bodies. It has to be full of love and liveliness. So what shall we do?

○ Express
Children are healthy because they know how to express their feelings. They do not possess duplicity. They express what they feel. They try what they like. Failure is a way of life and learning for them unless conditioned by adults to fear and avoid failures. Being hurt can be undone by forgiving and moving on in life. Children do not carry enmity in their hearts for long. Their innocence is the key to their happiness which comes from true expression of what they feel. Managing emotions is not curbing them but encouraging them to express themselves in the right manner to the right purpose.

○ Engage
Engagement with the environment through love, empathy and respect will ensure overall welfare and wellbeing. We need to harbor good feelings and oust ill feelings from our heart. We need to forgive from the heart and not only from our mind to reap the true benefits of forgiving. We need to manage our feelings so that we can interact with self and the world in a peaceful and loving manner.

- **Body**

  At various times I have heard that a healthy body harbors a healthy mind and heart. But I believe only a healthy mind and heart ensures healthy body. It works from inside to outside. Our physical body is the just the tip of the iceberg of our personality. If one's mind and heart is full of health and happiness, it will radiate and reflect in one's body. The gleam and glitter of a happy person is visible in his body. Noble thoughts and good feelings will lead to a body free from all illnesses and impurities.

  Suppressed feelings immediately affects our body in a negative way, suppressing our immune system and disturbing our various functions. A cluttered and confused mind leads the physical body into confusion and breakdown.

  A well-oiled and serviced car does not break down. It is designed to run efficiently under a trained driver. If we can ensure right maintenance and right driving, the car can run for long. The same is the case with one's body. The driver, our mind and heart needs to be in control of self. Positivity and passion will ensure that it never breaks under stress. The maintenance of our physical self through right nutrition, adequate rest and enough exercise is crucial to its longevity and liveliness.

  The body is a natural entity and needs to live naturally. A close association with nature and natural phenomena is required. We just need to maintain the right flow of material in and out of the body and within the body, whether it is air, water or food. What should we do?

○ Diet

The body understands nutrition in terms of carbohydrates, proteins, fats, oils, vitamins and minerals. We need to take care that we get these nutrients. We have to decide what to take care of …taste buds or our bodies.

○ Discipline

Happy living is always rooted in delayed gratification, by virtue of which we give away short term pleasure for long term and multiple benefits. Running everyday may be painful but it will save us from the pain of heart problems. Abstaining from sweets, spices and salt, may be difficult but it will prevent difficulties of bad health in long run.

• **Soul**

This is the most central and critical aspect of a human life. In fact, life is essentially our soul. It is this part of us, by virtue of which our journey of life as a human is a part of a larger movement of the cosmos. The tool of human body is blessed to us, for the divine journey of the life of our soul. It is due to this facet of ourselves that our journey's start and finish point are not in our hands.

Through our bodies, our soul is having a physical experience. Our body has to be seen in a different light if we want to live a healthy life. Our body is just the end result through which we can interact with the physical world. That is why, even a handicap person be healthier than others, if he knows his unique strength and capabilities. It is our relation and relevance to this world or our environment, which decides how healthy we are. The effective and efficient move on this journey of life itself is health.

Many articles and viewpoints are being written these days on managing stress, work-life balance, and so on. In dealing with the symptoms of problems we have forgotten to deal with the root causes or real problems underneath. We would not get tired or exhausted, if we are following and are in control of our passion, purpose or love. If we are living for a noble cause, we do not get stressed. Our work becomes our enjoyment and brings us enthusiasm and excitement. As per sport psychology, the intrinsic motivation and sheer joy one finds in playing the sport is crucial to one's performance. The body, mind, heart and soul all dance in perfect rhythm and synchrony. We flourish and bloom. So what should we do?

o   Find your true passion

o   Love what you do

Only healthy individuals can create healthy environment

The journey of life is a great experience if we have the vitality and vibrancy of health. Sickness and illness restricts our growth and development.

> Investing in health will produce enormous benefits.
> - Gro Harlem Brundtland

Can we enjoy a vacation, if we are ill? Then how can we enjoy our work, play and family under the stress of illness. We need to take care of not only our health, but also the overall environment we live in…our family, workplace and society.

Our health as leaders extends to our organization and society. Our strong physical body, sharp acumen and peaceful heart is reflected in the overall health of the organization or institution we work with or the country we live in. A disciplined individual who knows how to take care of his health will ensure a healthy environment around. He will not jump a red light, or take a bribe, because he knows that it will affect the health of his nation. It is not the external aggression or attacks which causes the deterioration of a country these days, but the internal imbalance and lack of stability in the governance. Health and education are the pillars of any great culture or country. The health of a culture is the result of summation of healthy individuals, where the whole contributes to parts, parts contributes to whole. A country with a nuclear weapons, but afflicted with lack of governance, and uneducated and undisciplined youth, is not a country worth living in. The health of a country or an individual is the ability to bloom and bear fruits of productivity and happiness for everyone. Not being a burden to self, but a boon and benefit for all the others around.

Our journey as an individual or an institution needs to be healthy, only then it can be enjoyed. We need to harmonize with everyone and everything else, to ensure a perfect health. It is our ability to co-exist and co-relate. Our journey of life is not only about us. It neither starts nor ends with us. It is our journey but it has to be a part of a bigger picture.

The human body has been designed to resist an infinite number of changes and attacks, brought about by its environment. The secret of good health lies in successful adjustment to changing stresses on the body.

- Harry J. Johnson

14

Communicate Spiritually

"Share your knowledge. It is a way to achieve immortality."

— Dalai Lama XIV

14

Communicate Spiritually

Being an avid adventurist, and through the variety of places I served in, I got a chance to see rich and varied types of terrain, culture and people. Be they deserts, mountains, valleys, rivers or forests, every time it left me awestruck by its perfection and precision. I felt as if the God wanted to convey or communicate His beauty and exquisiteness. When I saw the magnificent Burj Khalifa, the tallest structure ever made by human beings, I again felt that there is some kind of message or meaning in it, for the entire human race. It truly conveys mankind's never dying hunger for raising the bar and setting new standards.

I will reiterate the fact that the core of human race is beyond survival. We do not exist to survive but to evolve and endeavor. A beautiful structure like the Taj Mahal is just a manifestation of this aspect of human life. No one stays in it, it has no functional utility but serves only one purpose.... to communicate the human spirit or express its basic nature. We invent planes, rockets, submarines, satellites, computers, software, and so on, not for our existence but to express our nature, to communicate what we are made for or how we are made. We are here to communicate through our endeavors that we are on a journey beyond survival and safety. We take big risks, renounce everything, relate things, regulate ourselves, become restless, and revolt against ourselves, just to communicate something…our true selves. Life's journey itself is a communication … an event or experience of sharing what we believe in and what we stand for.

What is communication?

It is an act of sharing. We communicate to share our beliefs, ideas, values, dreams and so on. Certainly, communication is not (or only) speaking, presenting, debating and discussing. It is a bigger, wider and deeper term. It cannot be dealt with superficiality of one's diction and dialect, but by the profound and incisive role of character.

We are communicating each and every moment. We cannot escape communication. Being alive is itself is a form of communication. Whatever we are, gets expressed. Our life is a form of expression. Whatever we do in life: think, decide, act, speak, stand, intend and be, is all communication.

We cannot lie for long, to oneself or others. What we truly are and believe in is evident and we can only hide it for some time. There is a great benefit in being true to self and others around us. It relates to the last chapter, where I mentioned that health is a state of being in sync with the world around us. True, strength lies not in hiding facts but in being transparent and truthful. Insecurity breeds falsehood and breaks in communication. People who consider themselves to be an essential part of this world and interact with this world, are transparent. For them vulnerability is not an issue but a show of strength. Communication is not about sending and receiving messages, it is about being a part of the universe. It is about being an integral and indispensable part of the world around us through our unique talent and unique contributions.

How to communicate?

We do not need to bother about any speaking skills or presentation techniques. It is about being one's true self and moving on the journey of life with a purpose. It is our purpose and our way of life which communicates to others who we are. What we communicate to the world around is, lies in only one question: 'How do I live my life?'

When we enter some one's house, it speaks something about its owner. When we see a car or other such possessions, it speaks about its user. When

> "One should use common words to say uncommon things"
> — Arthur Schopenhauer

we enter an institution, it speaks about its values and vision. How every person interacts with us or even how the garden and buildings are maintained, conveys some overt messages. Even our globe, and its vastness and variety, communicates to us, about its creator.

Actually I am not a writer and this book is just an expression of my feelings and fascinations. One day, when I was just typing a few words while trying to clarify my thoughts to my friend, I got the idea of writing a book and helping people elucidate certain facts and facets of human life and its journey.

Since human beings are endowed with the special gift of speaking, we have lost the power of real communication. All animals communicate but they do not need human vocal chords to convey their feelings and frames of mind. At times, I have realized that we have all modes of communication, magnificence of vocabulary and well-mannered behavior but we still struggle to convey what we feel to the people we love most. Our lack or largeness of communication creates more confusion than clarity. At times, we communicate to confuse not only others but even our intra-communication or self-talk is not meaningful either. Often too much of communication is more harmful than good.

It is common to see in an organizational environment, trivial incidences or insignificant information being conveyed to higher authorities due to availability of faster and easier communication modes. People are losing ability, audacity and autonomy to solve problems.

Then what shall we do?

Communicate from the real you. As a trainer, I always recommend, 'We do not train or teach by what we say or do, but essentially by what we are', because we say or do, what we really are. One's real character and intentions can be sensed even by children.

Once a sage was asked to counsel a child to quit the habit of smoking. The sage agreed and asked for some time to accomplish this task. He came back after a few weeks and asked the child to quit smoking. When asked why he took so many weeks to do this simple task, he replied "How can I ask others to quit smoking without doing the same by myself?"

- **Authenticity**

Nothing appeals more than being authentic. By verbal communication, we just 'try' to convey what we want to convey. But 'what we are', conveys our complete existence with regards to our intention and identity. What we truly are, is communicated to the world around us, without our deliberate effort. It is sad to see that in today's world, we speak to hide what we really are or what our real intentions are. To communicate effectively, we need a relaxed state of mind or existence and let our true self "flow" out to others. We need to be true and sincere in our communication, and it has to flow from 'in to out', from our character to our environment. To practice this genuine communication, we need first, to be honest to self, regarding what we want from ourselves.

> "The great enemy of clear language is insincerity. When there is a gap between one's real and one's declared aims, one turns, as it were, instinctively to long words and exhausted idioms, like a cuttlefish spurting out ink."
> — George Orwell, Politics and the English Language

- **Accuracy**
At times, speaking less speaking conveys more than too much speaking. Most of the time less is more and slow is fast. We cannot hasten the process of a growth of a plant or of a child.

> "A solid answer to everything is not necessary. Blurry concepts influence one to focus, but postulated clarity influences arrogance."
> — Criss Jami, Salomé: In Every Inch In Every Mile

In the same way to communicate our ideas and intentions to others, we need to apply patience, for thoughts and ideas to germinate and grow in others' minds. We just need to be clear about the goal of the communication. We need to convey our concept with accuracy and assurance. Everything takes time. People are not easily convinced or persuaded by others. We just need to sow the idea in someone's mind and water it with right information and patience, and let the growth come from inside.

- **Affection**
Love and respect stand tall in the process of communication. No logic or reason can beat the language of love and respect. People yearn to feel important and appreciated. While communicating to people, we need to show our genuine affection for them. The affection should come from our heart and not from mind. We need to truly feel it, from our heart, for the people around us. That is

why communication from heart carries the biggest impact.

- **Action**

    Earlier too, I spoke on this aspect of human life and leadership. Action is the true form of communication. A small action conveys far more than a thousand words. Even teachers and trainers use the art of demonstrations to prove their point to a group of students. On our journey of life, what we do day-in day-out is our true self. In fact, our true identity is hidden in our daily agenda.

Many people question that how can they choose a life partner through a meeting of an hour. There is a point in it. But at the same time, it is also true that years of knowing each other can also ends up in a break-up in marriage. It is not the quantity of time but the quality of communication through which we know the other person. The art of communication goes far beyond exchanges of few bites of information.

Communication has to happen at all levels. On our journey of life, we need to communicate, and we do communicate, at every moment through

> The most important thing in communication is hearing what isn't said.
> -Peter Drucker

our body, mind, heart and soul. But the hustle bustle of today's life has deteriorated our capacity to discern these levels of communications. We have just lost the capacities to connect at these levels. In fact children are better in these capacities who communicate from the heart with great deal of authenticity.

How to communicate with self?

Self-communication is crucial to our personal leadership. Clarity within will lead to clarity without. We need to

> "The more of me I be,
> The clearer I can see."
> — Rachel Archelaus

first answer to ourselves, regarding the basic questions of life. We need to be clear in our self-concept before deriving concepts for this world. Today, we are in touch with all our friends, family and colleagues through a large number of gadgets and applications, but find it difficult to connect to self How to reach or relate to self in this busy world? Solitude. I have already spoken of this earlier. We need to find time away from the outside world to know the world within us.

How we communicate and act outside is dependent on the communication inside or with ourselves. The intra-communication should precede inter-communication. We need to have a clear communication with self before being able to commune with the outside world.

What do we achieve from Communication?

It is essentially a process of sharing the space and time with our environment. It is about creating relevance and relationship to the outside environment, consisting of people, places and purposes. It is about establishing peace within and outside ourselves. It leads us to co-exist with others on our journey.

> Communication - the human connection - is the key to personal and career success.
> -Paul J. Meyer.

All our actions, and non-actions, on our journey of life, communicates our worth and existential reasons. We need to move beyond the selfishness of survival and make our unique contributions to this world and beyond, to communicate our true worth.

All great lives, legends and legacies are forms of communications to the generations who are to come into existence. They communicate from where we have come and what shall be the direction of further endeavors and evolution. They have truly conveyed that we do not exist but evolve.

It helps us to deal with grey areas and ambiguous situations. Sessions of communication leads to clarifications and conclusions. It helps us to make sense out

> "Much unhappiness has come into the world because of bewilderment and things left unsaid."
> — Fyodor Dostoyevsky

of non-sense. When we can develop sixth sense or our intuition to ascertain and discern the situation, or when we can listen and speak more through silence, we reaches the true power of communication. At that time, we do not need the art of speaking and presentation. In fact, continuity and consistency in communication cements relationships, whereas gaps and breaches in communication breaks relationships.

We think in terms and limits of our vocabulary. As a human race, we have enlarged and enriched our vocabulary so much, to convey our deepest feelings. It is essential. However at the same time, apart from sharpness of mind we need the softness of heart to understand and unravel the hidden cues and nods.

To communicate effectively, we need to understand the subtle intelligent communication between the cells or systems of our bodies. They communicate and work in perfect coordination without any physical sounds. Since we are also a part of a bigger organism called humanity, we need to develop the same skill of communication for overall benefit. I always get mesmerized by the way vehicles moves on the roads. So many entities moving together without direct interaction, but still in perfect coordination!

To move ahead and farther on this journey of human life, we need to develop a deeper sense of communication. Our journey needs to be in sync and seamless with others too and as such ability to share space and time is crucial.

"What you are, and who you are should provide greater clarity about where you have been and where you are headed. Although one distinguishes spiritual from physical nature, the ultimate unification of the two is the consequence of the struggle for internal, external and eternal – peace."

— T.F. Hodge, From Within I Rise: Spiritual Triumph Over Death and Conscious Encounters with "The Divine Presence"

About the Author

Captain Mohit Tomar is an ex-army officer from Dehradun and an alumnus of the IIM. He lives for the cause of enlightenment and evolution of people, through his Leadership Training and Developmental programs. His wide range of experiences in military, corporate, consultancy and adventure brings great learning, rooted in real life experiences, to people.

He promotes self-directed, life-long learning as a natural way to live a well-accomplished life. According to him, life is the best teacher, provided we reflect and contemplate, to convert the events we go through, into meaningful learning experiences.

He believes that investment made in people will earn maximum returns, and justice and opportunity for all is a natural way to overall growth and well-being, for an organization, society or a nation.

He is an avid mountaineer and adventurer, and believes in challenging self through new and meaningful endeavors. He advocates people to live according to the values and vision of their lives. He urges his readers to, keep, keep, and keep searching for one's purpose in life, and create oneself by finding oneself.

Printed in the United States
By Bookmasters